HOW TO QUIT YOUR 9-TO-5 IN 90 DAYS

Your Guide to Build Residual Income for a Lifetime with Digital Products

Allen Brown

How To Quit Your 9-to-5 In 90 Days

Published by Build Our Kingdom Publishing, LLC

Printed in the United States of America

1st Edition September 2025 First Printing

ISBN for Paperback: 978-1-964203-32-4

Build Our Kingdom Publishing, LLC. 560 Main St, Stroudsburg, PA 18360

www.BuildOurKingdom.com

TABLE OF CONTENTS

INTRODUCTION

Why Resell Circle Is 100% Better Than Your 9-to-5

Let's get this straight from the beginning.

This book is not motivational fluff. This is a blueprint. This is a system. This is your way out.

How to Quit Your 9-to-5 in 90 Days and Build Residual Income for a Lifetime is not just a clever title — it's a mission. And if you follow what's in this book and lock in for the next 90 days, you can be done clocking in for someone else. Not maybe. Not possibly. You can be done. Period.

Now let's be real. Everybody wants to make money online. Everybody wants passive income. But most people never get there because they overcomplicate the process, chase shiny objects, or spend years building something from scratch that barely pays. That ends now. You're not here to struggle. You're here to tap into a system that already works.

That system is Resell Circle.

Resell Circle is 100% better than any job you've ever had. Why? Because with this platform, you don't trade time for money — you build assets. You don't wait for raises — you set your own price. You don't build someone else's dream — you build your own brand, your own customer base, and your own legacy.

Here's the big idea most people miss: **Resell Circle is the product.** Not just a tool. Not just a marketplace. A *done-for-you platform* you can offer to others — a platform that tracks customers to you for life, pays you in multiple ways, and lets you earn even when someone buys from another seller. Everything else — the LinkTree, the landing pages, the ability to upload digital products — is a byproduct of that core truth. Other companies sell you "done-for-you eBooks" or "done-for-you funnels." Resell Circle gives you a **done-for-you business platform** you can put in other people's hands and get paid from it, over and over again.

You want facts? Let's talk facts.

People all over the world are making money reselling digital products. They're flipping eBooks they didn't write. They're reselling templates, guides, planners, and checklists they didn't design. They're turning resale rights into full-blown businesses. The resale industry is already a multi-billion-dollar economy, and now you have a shot to own a piece of it.

With Resell Circle, you don't need to create anything to start earning. Read that again. You don't need to be a content creator. You don't need to make a product. You don't need to be an expert in design, writing, branding, or any of that. You don't even need a social media following.

You just need to share the system — and the system pays you.

And when we say "system," we mean a structure built to reward you across multiple streams. Customer ownership is for life. A single invite can turn into commissions you didn't "personally" sell, upgrades you didn't pitch, and residuals that stack month after month. That's not hype. That's how Resell Circle is engineered.

The Three Levels: Start Free, Scale Fast, Go Inner Circle

We've made the path simple:

Guest (Free): You can purchase products and earn 30% commissions when customers who are referred make purchases.

Bronze ($20/One time): Start with a one-time payment.. Access core tools like LinkTree and landing pages. As a Bronze member, you operate as an affiliate — promote other people's products and earn **30%** on sales. It's the simplest entry: no product required, no barrier to start sharing.

Platinum ($27/month): This is where the business opens up. You can sell *other people's* products right away. You can also sell *your own* products and keep **100%** on direct sales. If the marketplace sells your product for you, you still keep **60%**. Every customer you personally bring in is tagged to you for life — so when *they* buy from other sellers, you earn **30%**. On top of that, you earn **40% residual** every month from each Platinum person you refer, plus **10% overrides** from the activity of their customers. This is where leverage gets real.

Platinum Plus (~~$397~~ - $197 one-time + $27/month): Welcome to the inner circle. Get direct mentorship access, special calls, deeper support — and **$175 upfront** every time someone signs up as Platinum Plus through you, *plus* the ongoing residuals tied to their subscription. Platinum Plus is built for the member who wants guidance, speed, and high-ticket cash flow alongside monthly stacking.

Read those lines again and notice the pattern: **you're not just using a system — you're offering a system.** Shopify, ClickFunnels, Stan, Beacons and the rest help you *use* tools. Resell Circle positions you to *offer* the platform itself, keep customers for life, and participate in the value created across the marketplace. That's the difference. That's the edge.

How This Book Works: Two Phases to Freedom

To keep this simple — and powerful — this book is split into two phases.

Phase One: The 90-Day Execution Plan (Chapters 1–10).

We start by killing the job mentality and replacing it with ownership. Then we show you leverage, the habits that make this work, and the six ways you get paid. You'll set up your account, complete your training, invite your first five customers, and build momentum in Days 2–30. Next, you'll stack income in Days 31–60, define your avatar, master hashtags and targeting, write keyword-optimized captions that trigger search visibility, and close with a 90-day challenge that turns content into consistent conversions. This phase is step-by-step. No fluff. No guesswork. Just execution.

Phase Two: Beyond 90 Days — 10 Keys to Accelerate Your Freedom.

Once your engine is running, this second half is your accelerator. You'll sharpen the psychology of quitting your job, manage money like an owner, use storytelling that sells, avoid the biggest beginner mistakes, leverage community proof until you've stacked your own, pull from a 30-day content bank, treat the algorithm like your 24/7 employee, lock in a residual mindset, use the modern toolset (Canva, ChatGPT, Link hubs, Zoom), and keep momentum when life gets busy. These keys aren't required to start — they're how you scale and stay ahead.

Put simply: Phase One gets you moving. Phase Two multiplies everything you built.

The Promise

Here's what you can expect if you do the work:

- You'll understand why systems beat side hustles — and why Resell Circle is engineered for leverage.
- You'll learn exactly how each stream pays: **100%** on your products, **60%** when the marketplace sells yours, **30%** from your customers' purchases anywhere in the platform, **40% residuals** on Platinum subscriptions you refer, **10% overrides** from their customers, **$175 upfront** on every Platinum Plus activation through you and **$20** for every Bronze level activation through you..
- You'll see how to start fast (even with no product of your own), then transition into building products so you keep 100% on direct sales.
- You'll plug into training and community so you're never stuck — and you'll follow a daily plan that compounds into freedom.

And the best part? If all you did was share the platform itself — not even a product — you could still walk away with weekly commissions, stacked monthly residuals, and lifetime customer ownership. Most people never realize that. They think they need to build something first before they can earn. Not here. Not anymore.

Resell Circle is built for people who are ready to stop waiting and start earning. The only thing standing between you and a new lifestyle is commitment. If you show up, follow the instructions, share your link, and stay consistent — the income follows. And fast.

I'm not giving you empty promises. I'm giving you what worked for me and what's already working for people inside the community. I'm giving you the keys to a system that pays out in multiple directions. And I'm telling you right now — if you want to quit your job, if you want to make digital income real, if you're tired of struggling and watching other people win — this is your moment.

You don't need more potential.

You don't need more hype.

You need a system that works — and this one does.

So let's get to it. Phase One will walk you step by step through what to do, how to do it, and why it works. Phase Two will help you press the gas and never look back. I'm not here to inspire you. I’m here to equip you. You just have to show up and apply pressure.

By the end of this book, you’ll know exactly how to use Resell Circle to replace your 9-to-5.

Not theory. Not dreams. Execution.

Let’s go.

CHAPTER 1
BREAK THE CURSE — RENEW YOUR MINDSET

Before we get into strategies, commissions, or even the first step of building your business, we have to deal with the single biggest obstacle standing in your way: your mindset.

The truth is, most people don't fail in digital business because the system didn't work. They fail because they dragged the job mentality into entrepreneurship. They treat a business like a clock-in job, and then wonder why it never pays like one.

You know exactly what I'm talking about. That mindset where you wait for someone to tell you what to do. That mindset where you believe showing up is enough. That mindset that says, *"I'll try this for a week and see if it works."* No. That's not how ownership works. If you want freedom, you've got to think and move like an owner.

Jobs Train You to Obey. Systems Train You to Win.

A job conditions you to survive inside a system that doesn't belong to you. You're trained to follow schedules, hit deadlines, ask for permission, and perform tasks that don't lead to wealth — they just lead to the next paycheck.

But business isn't about survival. It's about growth.

If you step into entrepreneurship carrying that old job mindset, it will weigh you down. You'll hesitate when you should act. You'll play safe when you should move boldly. You'll spend more time doubting yourself than doing the work. And in the end, you'll give up — not because the opportunity wasn't real, but because you never shed the curse of employee thinking.

That's why this first chapter is so important. We're breaking the curse right here, before you go another step.

You're Not Waiting on a Check Anymore — You're Building One

Here's the difference: at a job, you're paid for showing up. At a business, you're paid for building something that works whether you show up or not.

Think about it. You can spend 40 hours at your job and still barely cover rent. But in the digital world, you can put in 10 focused hours building the right system, and those hours can keep paying you month after month. That's the shift.

This isn't about "side hustles." This isn't about chasing quick flips. This is about creating **residual income streams** — income that repeats, stacks, and compounds because you own the system that generates it.

When you start treating your actions like seeds instead of hours, you'll finally see how real wealth grows.

Hustle + Ownership = Freedom

Don't get it twisted. Freedom doesn't mean laziness. It still takes hustle. But hustle alone isn't enough — it has to be paired with ownership.

If you hustle inside someone else's system (like your job), your reward is capped. But if you hustle inside a system that belongs to you, the reward has no ceiling. That's the whole point of digital entrepreneurship.

When you combine daily action with a platform that multiplies your effort, you unlock leverage. And leverage is how people go from stuck in a paycheck cycle to controlling their income, their time, and their life.

That's the kind of hustle that sets you free.

The Excuses Have to Go

Now let's get real. If you're still sitting on excuses, this isn't going to work.

- *"I don't have time."* Everyone has 30 minutes a day. The question is whether you'll use it on TikTok scrolling or building your future.
- *"I don't know enough yet."* Nobody does when they start. The only way you learn is by doing.
- *"I need everything to be perfect first."* Perfection is procrastination in disguise.

Excuses are part of the job mentality. They're what employees use to justify staying stuck. But you're not here to stay stuck. You're here to break free.

Proof That It Works

Let's make this plain. People are already winning with this.

Some started with zero followers. Some didn't know how to upload a product. Some had no background in digital marketing. But what they all had in common was this: they took action.

They didn't wait until they "felt ready." They got ready by moving. They followed a system that was already built, and because they trusted the process, they started stacking results. $500 here. $1,000 there. Even $3,000 in a single month — from people who once thought digital income was impossible.

If it worked for them, it can work for you. The only difference is commitment.

The Reset Button

This chapter is your reset. Right here, right now, you decide you're done thinking like an employee.

No more waiting for permission. No more begging for hours. No more depending on HR or supervisors.

From here on out, you treat your digital business like what it is — your chance to build your own bag, your own customer base, and your own freedom.

Protect your time. Protect your energy. Protect your momentum. Because once you start acting like a boss, people notice. They'll ask questions. They'll follow you. They'll join you. And every move you make will compound.

The Path Forward

The rest of this book is going to give you everything you need to move from job-thinker to income-builder:

- In Chapter 2, we'll show you why systems beat effort every time — and how leverage makes money flow in ways jobs never can.
- In Chapter 3, you'll see exactly what it takes: commitment, consistency, and community.
- In Chapter 4, we'll break down all the ways Resell Circle pays you, step by step.
- And from Chapter 5 onward, you'll get a 90-day plan to quit your job and build residual income for a lifetime.

But none of that matters if you don't make the shift right here, in Chapter 1.

So, final word: You're the boss now. Own it. Move different. Think different. Build different.

This is your moment to kill the job mentality and start living like the builder you were meant to be.

CHAPTER 2 UNDERSTAND LEVERAGE — USE SYSTEMS, NOT JUST EFFORT

Why Effort Alone Has a Ceiling

Most people have been conditioned to believe that the only way to earn more money is to work more hours. If you want more income, you pick up overtime. If you want more stability, you work longer years. The problem with that mindset is simple: effort without leverage has a ceiling. Your energy runs out. Your time runs out. Eventually, no matter how hard you push, the paycheck plateaus. That is the curse of relying on effort alone. True wealth comes from leverage — from building something that continues to work when you're not working.

Active, Passive, and Residual Income

Think about income in three categories: active, passive, and residual. Active income is what most people know best. You work a shift, you get paid for that shift. If you don't show up, you don't get paid. Passive income happens when the work you did once keeps paying you later. Write a book, record a video, or design a product, and you can sell it over and over again without recreating it from scratch. Residual income is different — it's income that repeats on a cycle because you've tied yourself into a system. It shows up every month without you restarting the process. Residuals are what wealthy people chase, because they know consistent streams of income beat single bursts of cash every time.

How Resell Circle Creates Leverage

This is where systems come in. A system multiplies your effort so one action can ripple in multiple directions. If you spend an hour posting a product in a marketplace, that product isn't just visible for one day — it sits there for anyone to discover, buy, and resell again and again. If you share your link once, the system doesn't just track that person in the moment — it locks them to you for life. That means the action you took one time keeps producing. That is leverage. And that is the reason you cannot compare Resell Circle to other platforms.

Most side hustles and small businesses still tie income to your personal grind. If you sell candles on Etsy, you have to keep making candles. If you run a Shopify store, you have to constantly drive your own traffic and fulfill every order. Those aren't systems. They're jobs in disguise. Resell Circle, by design, is different. It is a marketplace where you don't just work — you offer a package. That package includes your own storefront, the ability to sell products directly, the ability to let others sell for you, and the ability to earn from every customer you refer, even if they never buy from you again.

Real-World Leverage in Action

Leverage shows up in several unique ways here. The first is lifetime customer ownership. When someone joins through your link, they're tagged to you forever. If they buy a product from you today and a completely different seller tomorrow, you still earn because the system recognizes they belong to your circle. That doesn't exist anywhere else. On other platforms, customers come and go. On Resell Circle, they're yours for life.

The second form of leverage is the marketplace multiplier. Imagine uploading one product and putting it out there. On a normal website, only you can sell it. On Resell Circle, the entire marketplace can pick it up and sell it too. That means while you're asleep or busy living your life, other people are driving sales back to you. They make their commission, and you make yours. Your effort is multiplied by the actions of others, without you having to lift a finger.

The third leverage loop is residual income. When you refer someone into the system, they may join simply to make money. If they choose to sell their own digital products through the platform, every sale they make strengthens your income too. While they're building their business, you're stacking 40% commissions from their monthly subscription. No other platform works this way — not Shopify, not your own website, not Stan, not Beacons. They may let you build, but they don't pay you while other people build. Here, the system rewards you for creating opportunity for others. That's true leverage — your circle grows, and with it, your income grows automatically.

Here's an example that makes it real. Let's say you share your referral link with a friend. They join the platform, look around, and decide to buy a product — not even from you, but from another seller in the marketplace. On any other platform, you would earn nothing from that. On Resell Circle, because they came in through you, you still earn a commission on that purchase. Your one action — sharing your link — created an income stream that pays you even when their money is flowing somewhere else. That's leverage.

Now let's take it a step further. Imagine that same friend doesn't just want to buy products, but also wants to upload their own. They pay for their subscription, they start uploading, and they begin selling in the marketplace. Every month they stay active, you earn 40% from their subscription. It doesn't matter if you personally sold anything that month. It doesn't matter if you created content. The system itself guarantees you residual income because you were the one who brought them into the circle. That is leverage on top of leverage. The person you referred builds their business, and you build your residuals.

Why Leverage Is the Path to Freedom

No other system combines these loops together. Stan and Beacons give you a link hub, but you don't earn if your customers go on to buy more somewhere else. Shopify and ClickFunnels give you tools to sell, but all the marketing and customer acquisition is on you. You can build a nice-looking site, but if no one visits it, you earn nothing. Even your own website won't do this — you can own the domain, pay for hosting, and upload products, but if your friend signs up to sell their own stuff, you don't get a monthly cut of their growth. Resell Circle stands alone because it allows you to not only use the system but also offer the system — and that's where the leverage truly multiplies.

Leverage is the key to quitting your job. You can't outwork a 9-to-5 by replacing it with another 9-to-5 disguised as entrepreneurship. You can't grind your way into freedom if every dollar still depends on you being awake and pushing. You need streams of income that branch out from your actions, and you need those streams to flow whether you're hustling that day or not. That's what leverage looks like, and that's why systems like Resell Circle exist.

This is why I said in the first chapter that you must kill the job mentality. Employees are trained to think only in terms of effort. Entrepreneurs think in terms of systems.

Leverage is what allows you to work less while earning more, to stop trading time for money and start stacking assets that keep paying you. The system is built. The opportunity is real. The only question is whether you'll use it.

In the next chapter, we'll talk about what it actually takes to succeed: the commitment, consistency, and community that transform leverage into lasting freedom. Because having a system is one thing — but showing up with the right habits is how you make it work.

CHAPTER 3
WHAT IT TAKES — COMMITMENT, CONSISTENCY, COMMUNITY

You Don't Need What You Think You Need

A lot of people come into digital business with the wrong picture in their head. They think they need to be a tech wizard, know how to code, have thousands of followers, or spend big money on ads. That's why so many quit before they even start. They convince themselves they don't have what it takes because they don't have the tools they *think* they need. The truth is, those things don't guarantee success at all. There are people with huge followings who never make a dime online, because they don't have a system or the right habits. And on the other hand, there are people with no following, no tech skills, and no ad budget who stack consistent income simply because they showed up and plugged into the system.

What you really need has nothing to do with flashy skills or big numbers. What you really need are three things: commitment, consistency, and community. If you lock those in, everything else falls into place. That's the difference between the ones who win with Resell Circle and the ones who quit too early.

Commitment: Treat It Like a Business, Not a Hobby

Commitment is the first requirement, because without it nothing else sticks. If you treat Resell Circle like a side project you'll "try out" when you feel like it, you'll get side-project results. And side-project results are usually pennies. But if you treat it like a business — even if you're only dedicating 30 minutes a day — your entire approach changes. You show up differently. You learn faster. You stick through the bumps.

This isn't about working 12-hour days. It's about making a decision that for the next 90 days, you're locked in. You're going to treat this system like your ticket out of the 9-to-5, and you're going to act accordingly. People who commit build momentum, and momentum multiplies results. Commitment also sets a standard for yourself. It means you're not negotiating with your excuses anymore. You've drawn a line in the sand and said, "This is happening."

Consistency: Small Daily Actions Beat Random Big Efforts

Consistency is where most people drop the ball. They'll work like crazy for a week, then disappear for two. Or they'll get fired up for one day, and then never touch it again. That's not how systems reward you. A system like Resell Circle is designed to multiply daily actions — not scattered bursts. Thirty minutes a day beats five hours once a month. Why? Because consistency creates visibility, visibility builds trust, and trust turns into sales and referrals.

Think of it like going to the gym. One workout won't change your body. But steady effort over 30 days, 60 days, 90 days — that's what transforms you. It's the same here. Post your link. Share your proof. Talk about your journey. Check your dashboard. Repeat. None of it takes hours, but doing it consistently builds the kind of momentum that can't be stopped. And the beauty is, once momentum kicks in, you need less effort to keep the results flowing. That's leverage at work — but it only activates if you stay consistent.

Community: Don't Try to Do It Alone

Community is the third piece, and it's the secret weapon most people overlook. Too many try to do business alone, isolated, figuring everything out the hard way. That's why they burn out. Resell Circle is built differently. It's a platform, but it's also a community. You're not just given a login and left on your own. You're plugged into mentorship calls, Resell Circle Academy trainings, and a network of people who are already doing what you're trying to do.

That community matters more than you realize. When you see proof of others winning, it kills doubt. When you hear from people who started just like you, it builds belief. And when you can ask questions, get feedback, and be part of a movement, it keeps you going when motivation dips. Community fills the gap between what you know now and what you'll need to know tomorrow. It's the difference between struggling in silence and building in confidence.

Here's a simple story to show you what I mean. One member came in with no social media presence and barely any tech knowledge. Instead of trying to figure it all out alone, they leaned on the calls, asked for advice, and followed the daily steps the community shared. Within 30 days, they were earning consistent commissions — not because they knew everything, but because they had the right support. That's the power of community, and it's baked into this system.

The Real Requirements for Success

So let's make it plain. You don't need coding skills. You don't need thousands of followers. You don't need ad money. You need commitment to treat this like your way out, consistency to keep showing up every day, and community to make the journey easier and faster. Those are the real requirements. Without them, even the best system won't save you. With them, even a beginner can stack income in 90 days.

In Chapter 1, we killed the job mentality. In Chapter 2, we explained leverage. Now in Chapter 3, you see what it truly takes to put it all into practice. These three things — commitment, consistency, and community — are the foundation of success. And the good news is, you already have access to all of them. You just need to use them.

In the next chapter, we're going to move from mindset and habits into the money itself. We'll break down exactly how Resell Circle pays you, step by step, through six different streams of income. If Chapter 3 shows you what it takes to win, Chapter 4 is going to show you why it pays to win big.

CHAPTER 4 THE SEVEN + STREAMS — HOW RESELL CIRCLE PAYS YOU

Why One Stream Isn't Enough

Most people never escape the paycheck cycle because they only know one way to earn: trading time for money. Even in the online world, most platforms keep you locked into a single income path. If you're selling on Shopify, you only get paid when you move your own products. If you're using Stan or Beacons, you only profit when someone clicks your link and buys directly from you. One stream of income might feel safe, but it's fragile. One slowdown, one missed sale, and your income dries up.

Wealth builders think differently. They understand that multiple streams of income protect you, free you, and create exponential growth. And that's exactly what Resell Circle delivers. Instead of locking you into one method of earning, the system now opens up seven-plus different streams, all designed to stack on top of each other.

The "plus" matters. When this book was first written, Resell Circle had six streams of income. But as the platform has grown, a new stream was added for Bronze members — and more opportunities will continue to be added as the system evolves. That's why we call it seven-plus ways to get paid. This isn't a static platform; it's a living, growing ecosystem where your earning potential expands over time.

In this chapter, we'll break down each of the seven streams step by step. You'll see how direct sales, marketplace leverage, lifetime commissions, residuals, overrides, high-ticket activations, and now Bronze referral commissions all work together to create a business that pays you upfront, pays you monthly, and keeps paying you as your circle grows.

Stream 1 & 2: Selling Your Own Products — and Letting Others Sell Them Too

The first stream is the simplest: sell your own digital products and keep 100% of the profit. Upload an eBook, a guide, a course, or a template, and every direct sale puts the full amount into your pocket. Unlike other platforms that take heavy cuts, this one doesn't touch your direct earnings. If you sell a $30 guide, you keep all $30. That's ownership.

But here's where it gets better. The second stream is something most people have never experienced before: getting paid when other people sell your products for you. On Resell Circle, you don't have to rely only on your marketing. The entire marketplace can take your product, promote it, and earn their commission — while you still pocket 60%. Imagine waking up to find someone across the country who sold your eBook while you were asleep. They get paid, you get paid, and your work continues to multiply. That is leverage in action, and it's why creators thrive here faster than anywhere else.

Stream 3: Lifetime Commissions from Your Customers

The third stream is where things really separate Resell Circle from everything else out there. When you bring in a customer, they're tagged to you for life. That means every time they buy a product in the marketplace — even if it's not yours — you earn 30%. You don't have to be the one who created it, you don't even have to be the one who sold it. Because the system recognizes that customer as part of your circle, you keep earning from them as long as they stay active.

Picture this: you share your link with a friend. They join, look around, and buy a course from another seller. On any other platform, that money is gone to you. On Resell Circle, you still collect your commission, because you're the one who brought them in. That's not a hustle — that's ownership. One action today sets up income opportunities that can pay you for months, even years.

Stream 4 & 5: Residuals and Overrides

The fourth stream is residual income from the Platinum and Platinum Plus members you refer. Every time they pay their subscription, you earn 40%. Think about what that means. Most businesses start every month at zero, hustling just to catch up. With residuals, you start every month already ahead. If you have five Platinum members active, you've got money already coming in before you even make another move. If you have fifty, you've built a base that feels like a second paycheck — except this one doesn't depend on a boss.

Then comes the fifth stream: overrides. This is when your customers start earning their own Platinum referrals, and you still get 10%. You're not just rewarded for your efforts; you're rewarded for helping others succeed. The system keeps crediting you because you were the one who built the circle in the first place. That means while they grow their income, yours grows too. No other digital platform rewards you for the growth of your customers. Here, the better they do, the better you do. That's what real community-driven wealth looks like.

Stream 6: Upfront $175 Platinum Plus Activations

Finally, the sixth stream is the one that delivers fast, high-ticket payouts: the Platinum Plus activation. Every time someone upgrades into Platinum Plus through your link, you collect $175 upfront. That's immediate, tangible cash flow that can change your week on the spot. And it doesn't stop there — you also continue earning from their subscription every single month. That combination of upfront plus residual income is rare. Most platforms give you one or the other. Resell Circle gives you both. It's instant reward plus long-term growth.

Here is a quick story that shows how powerful this is. One member referred a friend who was serious about building a business. That friend jumped straight into Platinum Plus. Instantly, the member earned $175. But then, the next month, they earned again on the subscription. And the month after that, the same. What started as a one-time referral turned into both immediate profit and ongoing passive income. That's the difference between a system that just pays once and a system that pays repeatedly.

Stream 7: Bronze Referral Commissions

Here's the newest upgrade to the system — and the reason we now call it **7+ ways to get paid.** Resell Circle is designed to grow with its members, and this addition proves it.

When you become a Bronze member, you unlock the ability to earn direct commissions every time you sign up another Bronze affiliate. As of this writing, the

Bronze level requires a one-time fee of **$27**, and you receive **$20** each time someone joins through you at that level. That's instant, upfront income simply for sharing the entry point of the system.

But here's where it gets exciting: this is only the beginning. Resell Circle is still young — less than 90 days live at the time of this edition — and as the platform grows, Bronze pricing may increase. For example, if Bronze upgrades to a $97 entry fee, you could be earning **$75–$80 commissions** per sign-up. That means the earlier you position yourself, the more upside you capture as the community expands.

This is why we say **7+ ways to get paid**. The streams you see here are just the foundation. As Resell Circle evolves, new income paths can and will be added, giving you more ways to build residuals, stack upfront commissions, and scale your circle of influence.

Why Seven+ Streams Matter

At this point, you can see why Resell Circle is different from every other platform out there. You're not relying on one stream of income, or even two. You're tapping into **seven-plus ways to get paid**, all working together. Some streams give you fast upfront cash flow, others build long-term monthly residuals, and others create leverage by letting the marketplace or your customers work on your behalf.

That combination means you don't start every month at zero. You start with momentum. You start with customers who are already tagged to you, subscribers who are already paying you, and new opportunities for growth being added as the platform evolves. That's why we say "seven-plus" — because this isn't the end. As Resell Circle grows, new earning paths will continue to roll out, stacking on top of what already exists.

To make this practical, here are **three case scenarios** that illustrate what's possible. These are not guarantees, but they show how the streams can combine in real numbers when you take action. Remember: you only earn commissions available at your current plan level (or higher after upgrading).

Scenario 1: Bronze Success

Bronze is a one-time $27 signup. As Bronze, you can resell the Bronze package and earn **$20 per Bronze sold.** We give you links and tools to promote.

- Example: You refer **10 Bronze signups**.
- Commission: 10 × $20 = **$200 one-time**

Note: Bronze also earns 30% on marketplace purchases from your customers; not included in this simple illustration.

Scenario 2: Platinum (Residuals + Bronze)

Platinum is $27/month. As Platinum, you can still sell Bronze ($20 each), and you earn **40% monthly** on each Platinum subscriber you refer.

- Example: In one week, you sell 5 Bronze and 2 Platinum.
- Bronze commission: 5 × $20 = **$100 one-time**
- Platinum residuals: 2 × (40% × $27) = 2 × $10.80 = **$21.60 per month**

Month 1 total: $100 (onc-time) + $21.60 (residual) = **$121.60**
Ongoing monthly residual: $21.60/month (so long as both Platinum subscribers remain active)

Alternative Illustration:
If you duplicate this effort the following month —

another 5 Bronze and 2 Platinum — here's what it looks like:

- Month 2 Bronze: +$100 one-time
- Month 2 new Platinum residuals: +$21.60/month
- Total residual base after two months: $43.20/month

Two-month earnings: $121.60 + $121.60 = **$243.20 total**, plus $43.20 in ongoing monthly residuals.

Scenario 3: Platinum Plus (High Ticket + Residuals)

Platinum Plus includes a one-time component and monthly subscription. As Platinum Plus, you earn **$175 per Platinum Plus signup**, plus 40% monthly on subscribers at the applicable tier.

- Example (Month 1):
  - Sell 2 Platinum Plus → 2 × $175 = **$350 one-time**
  - Refer 10 Bronze → 10 × $20 = **$200 one-time**
  - Enroll 3 creators on $27/month plan → residuals: 3 × (40% × $27) = **$32.40/month**

Month 1 total: $350 (Plus) + $200 (Bronze) + $32.40 (residual) = **$582.40**
Month 2 residual: $32.40 (assuming all 3 remain active)
Two-month cumulative: $582.40 + $32.40 = **$614.80**

Alternative Illustration:
If you duplicate this effort in Month 2 — another 2 Platinum Plus, 10 Bronze, and 3 new creators — here's what happens:

- Month 2 one-time commissions: $350 + $200 = **$550**
- Month 2 new residuals: +$32.40/month
- Residual base after two months: $64.80/month

Two-month cumulative: ($582.40 + $614.80) = **$1,197.20**, plus $64.80 ongoing monthly residuals.

The Bottom Line

These scenarios are simple illustrations, but they show you the power of stacking streams. Whether you're starting at Bronze, building residuals at Platinum, or leveraging high-ticket activations at Platinum Plus, the system is designed to reward your effort over and over. And as more income streams are added, your circle only gets stronger.

The Big Picture

By now you can see why this chapter matters. Mindset (Chapter 1) gets you ready. Leverage (Chapter 2) shows you why systems beat effort. Commitment, consistency, and community (Chapter 3) give you the foundation. And now in Chapter 4, you've seen the reward: six powerful streams of income that stack on top of each other to build a business that doesn't collapse if one piece slows down. That's how real wealth is created — not from one hustle, not from one sale, but from multiple streams flowing together.

In the next chapter, we're going to get practical. You'll learn how to set up your account on Day 1 so you can start tapping into these streams immediately. No fluff, no waiting — just the exact steps to go from signing up to earning in your first 48 hours.

CHAPTER 5
YOUR DAY 1 SETUP — TRAINING BEFORE EARNING

Why Training Comes First

When you start a new job, the very first thing they do is train you. They don't just throw you into the role and hope you figure it out. You shadow someone, watch the videos, or go through the manual. Why? Because training builds confidence. Training equips you to perform at your best. The same thing applies here. If you want to treat this like the business that replaces your job, you can't skip the foundation. Too many people rush past training because they're so eager to "make money now." But here's the truth: the fastest way to make money is to learn the system first. The more you know about what Resell Circle is and how it works, the easier it is to talk about it, share it, and invite others. Training gives you the words. Training gives you the clarity. Training even helps you figure out your avatar—the exact type of person you should be sharing this with. You wouldn't start a new position without learning what's expected of you, so don't start your new business without learning how to use the tools.

The Setup Checklist Every New Member Must Do

Before you dive into training, there are three simple things every new member should knock out immediately. These might feel small, but they're the foundation of your business presence inside the community. First, confirm your email. This is about trust. It verifies your account and connects you properly to the system so you don't miss updates, referrals, or customer alerts. Second, upload a profile picture. People want to see who they're connecting with. This isn't about being perfect or professional. It's about showing up as a real person. A blank profile makes you look invisible; a face makes you relatable. Third, introduce yourself to the community. This step might feel uncomfortable, but it sets the tone. You're not here to hide. You're here to build. A simple hello, a short line about who you are, and maybe why you joined is all it takes. The moment you do that, you're plugged into a network of people who want to see you win. These three steps might take you less than 10 minutes, but they create a sense of ownership. They tell the system—and yourself—that you're serious. You're not a guest anymore. You're part of the circle.

Complete Your Free Mentorship Training (Six Modules)

Right after your setup, dive into the free mentorship program. The platform gives you six core modules designed to help you understand the system, the opportunity, and the flow of how everything works together. You don't need to memorize anything—just watch, take notes if it helps, and let the structure do its job. The more you absorb here, the faster everything else makes sense. Treat the modules like your shortcut to confidence. You'll learn what the platform does, how to talk about it without sounding salesy, and how to identify the people who will benefit most from what you offer. That "who" matters. When you can picture your avatar clearly, sharing becomes natural because you're simply pointing the right people to the right solution. This is required learning, just like any job. The difference is, here your learning turns into income. Finish the modules before you start promoting, and you'll avoid the confusion that slows most beginners. Training first, then action. That's how you build momentum without burning out.

Invite Your First Five Customers

After setup and training, your very first milestone is simple: invite your first five customers. Not 50, not 500—just five. This is where momentum begins. These don't all have to be paying customers yet. The goal is to get them into the system so they're tagged to you. Once they're inside, the platform goes to work. Automated emails are sent on your behalf. They'll see the products, the training, and the opportunities. You don't have to do the heavy lifting—the system does it for you. Why five? Because five is enough to give you proof that this works. Five is enough to get you comfortable sharing your link. Five is enough to start conversations. And often, five is enough to trigger your first commission. That first win builds belief. And belief builds consistency. Before you know it, your circle starts to grow. Here's the exciting part: the system will track those first five for you as a visible milestone. You'll be able to see them in your dashboard and check off that goal. That makes it a game. You'll know when you've hit it, and you'll know when it's time to push for the next five. That's how businesses grow—one small goal at a time. One new member followed this exact path: setup, modules, five invites. They didn't overthink it.

They didn't wait for the "perfect" pitch. They shared their link with people they already knew. Within a week, one of those five upgraded, and just like that, they had their first commission. It wasn't luck. It was training plus action. Your Day 1 is simple but powerful: confirm your email, upload your picture, introduce yourself, complete the six modules, and invite your first five customers. If that sounds basic, that's the point. The biggest mistake people make in digital business is overcomplicating the start. They think they need logos, branding, or endless prep. They don't. They need action. Day 1 isn't about making thousands. It's about proving to yourself that you've started. It's about building momentum. And it's about laying a foundation for the weeks to come. Once you've hit those first five customers, everything else becomes easier. You've broken the ice. You've taken the first step. In Chapter 6, we'll expand on what happens in the next 30 days—how to build, share, and learn so your first five turns into your first fifty. But it all starts here. If you want freedom, don't skip training. If you want results, don't avoid the basics. And if you want to quit your job in 90 days, don't hesitate on Day 1. Do the setup. Do the training. Invite your first five. And watch what happens next.

CHAPTER 6
DAYS 2–30 — BUILD, SHARE, AND LEARN

Start With What You Already Have

The biggest mistake new members make after setting up their account is waiting. They think they need to build the perfect product, craft the perfect brand, or line up the perfect strategy before they can start. That hesitation kills momentum. The truth is, you don't have to wait — you already have products in your profile the moment you join. That means on Day 2 you can start sharing. You can share those built-in products or grab any product from the marketplace and begin offering it right away. By doing this, you begin creating activity, clicks, and conversations before you've even thought about creating your own digital product. The system is designed this way for a reason. It gives you the ability to move immediately so you don't stall out. Success favors speed, and the sooner you share, the sooner the system can start working for you.

At the same time, keep in mind the bigger goal: eventually, you'll want to have your own digital products inside the platform. That's how you unlock 100% direct commissions. But while you work toward that, don't leave money on the table. Use what's already there. Share other people's products, share the ones pre-loaded into your profile, and let the marketplace work for you. This isn't about waiting until you're "ready." It's about starting where you are and letting the system multiply your actions.

Done For You Products and Your First Uploads

One of the easiest ways to begin is by using Done For You products. These are digital files that are already created — eBooks, guides, courses, planners, or templates that come with resell rights. Instead of spending weeks building something from scratch, you can take one of these products and immediately offer it through your storefront. Done For You means the hard part is finished; your job is to share, present, and earn. That's why so many beginners get their first commission without ever writing a single page or recording a single video.

Resell Circle also gives you more than just products. In your free bonus area, you'll find books and resources that teach you how to make your own digital products. You don't need to dive deep into that right now, but know this:

the sooner you learn to create, the sooner you'll put yourself in position to earn 100% on every direct sale. There's a difference between sharing what's already made and owning your own file. Done For You is your quick start, but building your own products is your long-term play. Both are available, and both matter.

What Digital Products Really Are

When people hear "digital products," sometimes they overcomplicate it. They imagine complex apps, expensive designs, or things only experts can make. That's not the case. A digital product is simply something valuable that can be delivered as a file. Think of a PDF ebook or checklist. Think of an MP4 video course or tutorial. Think of an MP3 audio lesson or podcast-style training. Think of templates, journals, or planners that people can download and use. Those are all digital products. They're simple, powerful, and highly scalable.

If you're a Platinum Plus member, you also have the ability to upload two training courses to start. That gives you even more room to grow, because courses are one of the most in-demand product types online. The point is, digital products aren't mysterious. They're everyday tools people already buy and consume. The only difference is, now you're the one offering them instead of just being a customer. Once you understand how simple they are, you'll realize you can create, upload, and start earning without needing years of experience.

Stay Plugged Into Training and Community

During these first 30 days, one of the smartest moves you can make is to stay connected. Don't try to do this alone. You have access to free Zoom mentorship calls where you can ask questions, hear from leaders, and see proof from other members who are winning. You also have access to Resell Circle Academy on Skool, where trainings, updates, and resources are shared. Use them. The people who plug in regularly learn faster, apply better, and stick around longer.

Think of it this way: a business owner who never trains their team is asking for failure. In the same way, an entrepreneur who ignores community support is setting themselves up for burnout. Your growth in these next 30 days isn't just about sharing links. It's about learning, connecting, and building confidence through mentorship and community. Stay plugged in, and you'll never feel lost.

Position Yourself on Social Media

Your business can't grow if people can't find you. That's why during Days 2–30, it's crucial to set up your social media presence properly. This doesn't mean you need to post flashy content or dance on TikTok. It means you need to position yourself so that every time someone visits your profile, they know exactly where to go. The easiest way to do this is with your invite link or your LinkTree. Put it front and center. Make it visible.

And here's the rule: your top three links should always lead back to Resell Circle in some way. Whether it's your direct invite link, your storefront, or the free training, those top three slots are prime real estate. Don't waste them on random links. Use them to funnel people back into the system where they can become your customers. Social media is your front door, and your links are the pathway into your business. Treat them like it.

Apply the Module 6 Action Plan

Finally, let's talk about execution. Training is valuable, but it only pays off if you act. Module 6 lays out the simple formula: one hour a day. That's it. You don't need to spend 10 hours glued to your phone. You need one focused hour where you're intentional. Inside that hour, make 20 meaningful comments on social media to get visibility. Post at least once a day to show up in front of your audience. And if you're ready to take it further, go live. Lives are powerful because they build instant trust.

If the idea of going live scares you, you're not alone. That's why the platform gives you the free *Show & Tell, Don't Sell* training. It comes as an ebook, an audiobook, and even a worksheet inside the free video training section. That worksheet is a blueprint. It tells you exactly how to structure your live so you don't freeze up. You just follow the outline and share your story. That's it. The more you do it, the more natural it feels. And the more natural it feels, the faster your results stack up.

Build, Share, Learn

That's the theme of your next 30 days: build, share, and learn. Build by using the tools and products already in your profile. Share by putting your invite links in front of people every day. Learn by staying plugged into Zoom calls, trainings, and community. Do these three things for 30 days and you'll have proof that this works. You'll have your first customers. You'll have your first commissions. You'll have your first story to tell.

The first 30 days aren't about perfection. They're about movement. Small, daily steps create momentum. And momentum creates results. So don't overthink it. Share the products you already have. Work toward creating your own. Plug into the community. Position yourself online. And apply the Module 6 formula every day. If you can do that for one month, you'll be ahead of 90% of people who start businesses and quit before they even get moving.

In the next chapter, we'll look at Days 31–60 — where you go from proving it works to stacking your income. That's when you'll learn how to use higher-license products, build your community, and start multiplying your results. But first, lock in these 30 days. They are your foundation. And if you get them right, the rest of the journey becomes a whole lot easier.

CHAPTER 7
DAYS 31–60 — STACK YOUR INCOME

Why the First 30 Days Matter

Your first 30 days laid the foundation. You confirmed your email, uploaded your picture, introduced yourself to the community, completed your training modules, and invited your first five customers. You also started sharing the products that were already in your profile, which gave you activity, visibility, and your first taste of how the system works. That wasn't about perfection. It was about movement. And now you've got momentum.

The purpose of the next 30 days isn't to start over. It's to stack. If the first month proved the system works, the second month is about multiplying your opportunities. That's where your income begins to stretch. This chapter is going to show you exactly how to stack: by understanding higher-license products, growing your customer list inside the platform, showing your results publicly, inviting creators to strengthen the circle, and creating your first lead magnet.

Understanding Higher-License Products

By now you know the basics: you can share the products in your profile or promote other people's products from the marketplace. That's your entry point. But Resell Circle also gives you access to different kinds of products that come with licensing rights. These licenses give you more flexibility and more earning power, because you're not just selling a product—you're offering ownership rights.

Here's the breakdown: Resale Rights (RR) allow you to resell a product as-is. You don't change it, you don't rebrand it—you just sell it and keep the profit. Master Resale Rights (MRR) take it further. With MRR, you can resell the product *and* pass the resale rights to others. That means whoever buys from you can also resell it and make money themselves. It's a powerful upgrade because it adds another layer of value. Finally, Private Label Rights (PLR) give you full creative control. You can edit the product, change the cover, rebrand it, and even claim it as your own. That's the highest level of flexibility because it lets you put your name on it and turn it into something unique.

Each of these licenses increases the value of what you're offering. Resale Rights are simple and straightforward. Master Resale Rights give buyers more earning potential. Private Label Rights give you ownership and branding power. The more value a license carries, the more you can charge. You don't have to dive deep into licenses on Day 31, but it's important to know they exist. They're one of the easiest ways to stack your income beyond just basic product sharing.

Growing Your Customer List Inside the System

A lot of marketers will tell you to build an email list. That's great advice, but it's not where you need to start right now. Resell Circle already gives you the ability to build a customer list inside the system—and that's where your focus should be. Every person you invite, whether they join free or paid, becomes part of your customer base. And remember: every customer is tagged to you for life.

This is where stacking begins. In your first 30 days, your goal was five customers. In Days 31–60, your goal should be to double and triple that. Aim for 15, 20, or even 25 customers inside the system. Why? Because every customer unlocks multiple streams of income. Some will buy products directly. Some will buy from other sellers. Some will upgrade to Platinum or Platinum Plus. Every move they make grows your income because they're part of your circle.

So don't think small here. Make it your mission to grow your in-system customer list every single week. That's your foundation for residuals, overrides, and long-term ownership.

Show Your Results (Proof Sells)

If you want to build credibility fast, share your results. Proof sells. And the best part is, your results don't have to be massive to matter. Screenshot your dashboard showing activity. Post about your first commission. Share a story about how you set up your profile or invited your first five customers. Even the smallest proof points tell people, "This is real, and it works."

And don't just post—go live. Going live is one of the most powerful ways to build trust because it's raw, unscripted, and authentic. You're not trying to be a professional presenter. You're simply showing what you're doing and letting people see your journey. That's why we push the *Show & Tell, Don't Sell* formula. Don't pressure people. Don't sound like a salesperson. Just show them what you're learning, what you're earning, and what the system is doing for you. Let the system do the selling. Your job is to show.

Every time you share proof, you create belief. And belief multiplies your circle faster than anything else.

Invite Creators to Upload Products

Up to now, your focus has been mostly on customers. That's good—but if you really want to stack, you have to start looking at creators too. Creators are the lifeblood of this space. They upload products, expand the marketplace, and bring more value to the system. And when you invite a creator, you unlock residual income, because their subscription feeds into your circle every month.

This is where you begin to see the difference between Resell Circle and every other platform. On Shopify, if someone else builds a store, you don't earn from it. On ClickFunnels, if someone else launches a funnel, you don't benefit. But here, when creators come in through you, their success adds to your success. That's leverage.

In Chapter 8 we'll cover how to find exactly who your perfect creator avatar is. For now, just know this: part of stacking your income is connecting with other creators and showing them why Resell Circle is the platform they need. Every creator you bring in is a long-term win for you.

Create Your First Lead Magnet

One of the smartest ways to grow your circle in this phase is by creating your first lead magnet. A lead magnet is a freebie you give away to attract people. It could be a short ebook, a checklist, or a quick guide that solves a small problem for your audience. And here's the good news: you don't have to write it from scratch. You can use ChatGPT to help create it. Just tell it your topic, and in minutes you'll have content that you can turn into a PDF.

What kind of lead magnet works? Think simple. "10 Digital Marketing Tips for Beginners." "How to Make Your First Digital Sale." "Five Ways to Earn From Digital Products." Anything that catches attention and speaks to the struggles of your avatar will work. By Day 60, your goal should be to have at least one free lead magnet uploaded into the system and connected to your free lead page. That way, when someone clicks, you're not just hoping they buy something—you're capturing them as a customer and giving them value immediately. That one freebie can turn into dozens of long-term customers.

The Stacking Formula

Stacking your income isn't about chasing ten different directions at once. It's about building layers. In your first 30 days, you proved the system works. In the next 30 days, you expand. You learn about licenses and higher-value products. You grow your in-system customer list. You share your results publicly. You invite creators. You create your first lead magnet. These steps stack on top of each other. They multiply. And they push you closer to financial freedom.

By the end of Day 60, you should feel confident. You've gone from setup to sharing to stacking. You've grown your circle, proven the system, and added new tools to your strategy. And now you're ready for the next big step: defining your avatar. In Chapter 8, we're going to break down exactly who your audience is, where to find them, and even the hashtags you should be using to attract them. That's when your growth goes from stacking income to scaling influence.

CHAPTER 8
DEFINE YOUR AVATAR AND FIND THEM EVERYWHERE

Why Your Avatar Matters

Not everyone online is your customer. If you try to talk to everyone, you end up connecting with no one. That's where the concept of an avatar comes in. Your avatar is your ideal customer — the person you're speaking to every time you post, go live, or send out a link. The clearer you are about who they are, what they want, and where they spend time online, the easier it becomes to attract them into your circle. Without an avatar, your message is scattered. With one, your message is sharp, focused, and magnetic.

When you know your avatar, you stop feeling like you're chasing random people. Instead, you start feeling like you're having conversations with the exact people who are already looking for what you're offering. That changes everything.

Defining Your Avatar

Defining your avatar doesn't have to be complicated. Start with a simple formula:

- **Who they are**: Are they beginners in digital marketing? Are they employees looking for side income? Are they creators looking for a platform to sell?
- **What they want**: Freedom, extra income, a system to resell products, or a way to create their own.
- **What they struggle with**: Lack of followers, lack of tech skills, job stress, burnout, or not knowing how to start.
- **Where they hang out**: TikTok, Instagram, Facebook groups, YouTube, or Twitter/X.

The more you fill in these blanks, the clearer your picture becomes.

If you're unsure where to start, use ChatGPT as your assistant. Try a prompt like this:

Prompt: "Help me define a customer avatar for digital products and digital marketing. Include demographics, goals, struggles, and buying motivations."

In less than a minute, you'll have a detailed sketch of who your ideal customer is — and you can refine it as you learn more about your audience.

Where to Find Your Avatar

Once you know who you're looking for, the next question is: where are they spending their time? The good news is, your avatar is already out there. You just have to go where they are.

- **Facebook** → Look for groups about digital marketing, online income, side hustles, and passive income. Join the conversations, not just to sell, but to build presence.
- **TikTok** → Search for creators who talk about side hustles, PLR, ebooks, or digital products. Watch what content is trending and add your voice to the space.
- **Instagram** → Explore hashtags like #DigitalProducts and #PassiveIncome. Post reels and carousels using these tags so your content shows up in their feed.

- **Twitter/X** → Search hashtags like #makemoneyonline or #financialfreedom. Join threads and respond with value.
- **YouTube** → Look for channels teaching digital business and products. Comment on videos, share your thoughts, and connect with viewers in the comment section.

The goal isn't to be everywhere. The goal is to know where your avatar is most active and then show up consistently in that space.

Hashtags That Attract Your Avatar

Hashtags are like highways that lead people to your content. Use the right ones, and your posts will get discovered by the exact audience you're trying to reach. Here's a list of 45 hashtags you can start using across TikTok, Instagram, and Twitter:

#DigitalMarketing

#DigitalProducts

#OnlineBusiness

#PassiveIncome

#MakeMoneyOnline

#FinancialFreedom

#SideHustle

#WorkFromHome

#EbookBusiness

#PLR

#ResaleRights

#MasterResaleRights

#PrivateLabelRights

#EntrepreneurMindset

#OnlineIncome

#EarnWhileYouSleep

#MoneyMoves

#HustleSmart

#DigitalEntrepreneur

#OnlineMarketingTips

#BuildYourBrand

#ContentCreatorLife

#StartYourBusiness

#FreedomLifestyle

#DigitalCoaching

#OnlineOpportunities

#MarketingForBeginners

#DigitalMarketingTips

#SmallBusinessOnline

#WorkAnywhere

#ResidualIncome

#ScalingOnline

#GrowYourBusiness

#MakeMoneyWithEbooks

#AutomatedIncome

#BuildWealthOnline

#CreatorEconomy

#LaptopLifestyle

#SocialMediaMarketing

#OnlineSelling

#DigitalDownloads

#MoneyFromHome

#FutureOfBusiness

#CreateAndSell

#EbookMarketing

#HustleFromHome

Mix these. Don't just use the big ones like #MakeMoneyOnline (which millions of people follow) —

balance them with niche hashtags like #PLR or #ResaleRights where your avatar is actively searching for answers.

How to Attract Them

Once you know where your avatar is, the next step is to pull them in. Here's how:

- **Show & Tell** → Share your results, your journey, and your activity. Don't try to sell — just show.
- **Comments Strategy** → Spend time leaving thoughtful comments on posts and videos in your niche. This pulls people back to your profile.
- **Optimize Your Links** → Your invite link or LinkTree should be visible in your bio. Make sure your top three links always point back to Resell Circle.
- **Stay Consistent** → Your avatar won't find you if you post once and disappear. Show up daily, even with small posts.

The more visible you are, the more your avatar recognizes you as the person with the solution they need.

Use ChatGPT to Speed Up Content

You don't have to create everything from scratch. ChatGPT can save you time and give you ideas you wouldn't have thought of. Here are four ready-to-use prompts to help you attract your avatar:

1. **TikTok ideas** → "Write me 5 TikTok video ideas that show beginners how to start selling digital products."
2. **Instagram captions** → "Create 3 Instagram captions about building passive income with digital products. Make them friendly and motivating."
3. **Facebook engagement** → "Give me 10 Facebook group discussion starters about online income and digital marketing for beginners."
4. **Caption rewrites** → "Rewrite this caption in a way that sounds more engaging and conversational: [insert your caption here]."

These prompts turn ChatGPT into your personal content assistant. The more you use it, the easier it becomes to show up daily without running out of things to say.

From Avatar to Captions (What's Next)

By the end of Day 60, you should have a clear picture of your avatar, know where they hang out, and start showing up with content they can relate to. That's how you turn random activity into focused growth. Your job now is to attract the right people consistently, and the steps in this chapter are your playbook for doing exactly that.

In the next chapter, we're going to go even deeper into what actually makes your content stick: **captions.** Social platforms are shifting toward AI that tracks what's written in your posts and even what's said in your videos. That means captions and keywords aren't just optional — they're critical. In Chapter 9, you'll learn how to write captions that use the right keywords, attract the right searches, and get your posts in front of the people who need them. Your avatar is step one. Optimized captions are step two. Put them together, and your visibility explodes.

CHAPTER 9
HOW TO WRITE THE PERFECT CAPTIONS IN YOUR SOCIAL MEDIA

Why Captions Matter More Than Ever

Social media has changed. A few years ago, you could post a picture, throw a few hashtags on it, and hope people found it. That doesn't work anymore. Platforms like TikTok, Instagram, and YouTube now use AI to analyze *every word you say and every word you type.* Your captions and your spoken words are being transcribed and indexed behind the scenes. That means the algorithm isn't just looking at hashtags — it's scanning your captions and matching them with what people are searching for.

If your captions are weak, vague, or off-topic, you disappear into the noise. But if your captions are sharp, keyword-rich, and aligned with what your avatar is looking for, the algorithm puts you in front of more people. In other words, captions are no longer optional—they are the engine that drives visibility.

The Role of Keywords in Captions

Keywords are simply the words and phrases your audience is already typing into search bars. If someone wants to learn how to sell ebooks, they're searching "how to make money with ebooks" or "ebook business for beginners." If they want passive income ideas, they're searching "best side hustles online" or "how to make passive income."

Your captions need to echo these exact phrases. Think of it like SEO for social media. When you include keywords naturally in your caption, you're telling the algorithm, "This post is about [topic], so show it to people searching for [topic]." That's how your posts end up in front of the right people without you spending money on ads.

Here's a simple rule: hashtags bring attention, but keywords keep you visible. Use both together and your content has double the power.

How to Write Captions That Rank

So how do you write captions that actually work? Follow this formula:

1. **Hook your reader in the first line.** This is the scroll-stopper. Ask a question, drop a bold statement, or call out your avatar directly. Example: "Want to quit your 9-to-5 in the next 90 days?"
2. **Use keywords naturally.** Don't stuff your captions like a robot. Instead, write the way you talk, but sprinkle in phrases your audience searches for. Example: "Selling digital products is the fastest way to build passive income online."
3. **Add value in 2–3 sentences.** Share a quick tip, insight, or story. Example: "You don't need tech skills, a huge following, or ad money to start. With resale rights products, you can sell ebooks, templates, or courses that are already done for you."
4. **End with a call to action.** Tell them what to do next. Example: "Click the link in my bio to grab your free guide and start today."

That's it. Four parts. Hook, keywords, value, CTA. Short captions can follow the same structure in fewer words. Long captions can expand it into a mini-story. Either way, this formula keeps your posts optimized.

Examples of Optimized Captions

Let's look at some practical examples using keywords from the hashtags we listed in Chapter 8:

- **For TikTok/Instagram Reels**:
- "Digital products are the future. If you've ever thought about creating passive income from home, this is your moment. I started with resale rights ebooks and turned them into a business. You can too. #DigitalProducts #PassiveIncome #MakeMoneyOnline"
- **For Facebook/Instagram Posts**:
- "Tired of side hustles that take too much time? Digital products give you a way to make money online without starting from scratch. With resale rights, you can sell ebooks, templates, or courses that are already done for you. Start today with your free training inside my link."

- **For Twitter/X**:
- "Building passive income online isn't about luck. It's about systems. Digital products + resale rights = financial freedom. Start with ebooks, templates, or guides. #OnlineBusiness #PassiveIncome #DigitalMarketing"

Notice how each caption includes natural keywords: digital products, resale rights, passive income, online business, ebooks. These are search-friendly, but they still sound conversational.

Using ChatGPT to Craft Captions

You don't have to write every caption from scratch. ChatGPT can be your caption factory. Here are prompts you can copy and paste:

1. **Short captions with keywords** → "Write me 5 short captions under 50 words that include the keywords 'digital products,' 'passive income,' and 'online business.' Make them sound natural."
2. **Hook ideas** → "Give me 10 attention-grabbing first lines for captions about quitting a 9-to-5 and building passive income."

3. **Platform-specific captions** → "Write 3 TikTok captions, 3 Instagram captions, and 3 Twitter posts about selling resale rights ebooks online."
4. **Rewrite for clarity** → "Here's my caption: [paste caption]. Rewrite it with stronger keywords and a clearer call to action."

The key is to train ChatGPT with your focus. Tell it the keywords you want included, the tone you want to use, and the platform you're posting on. In seconds, you'll have captions optimized for both humans and algorithms.

Common Mistakes to Avoid

While writing captions, avoid these traps:

- **Being too vague.** "Make money online" by itself isn't enough. Add context: "Make money online by selling resale rights ebooks."
- **Keyword stuffing.** Don't cram a dozen phrases into one caption. Keep it natural.
- **No CTA.** If you don't tell people what to do, they'll scroll right past. Always give direction.

- **Talking to everyone.** Remember your avatar from Chapter 8. Write captions like you're talking to one person, not the whole internet.

Your Daily Caption Practice

Here's what to do moving forward:

- Every day, write at least one caption using the formula: Hook + Keywords + Value + CTA.
- Keep a list of 10–15 keywords relevant to your avatar. Use them in rotation.
- Test short captions vs. long captions. See which your audience responds to most.
- Use ChatGPT to brainstorm when you feel stuck.

The more you practice, the sharper your captions will get. Within weeks, you'll notice your posts reaching more people, attracting better conversations, and pulling more customers into your circle.

From Captions to Conversion (What's Next)

By mastering captions, you're no longer throwing content into the void. You're strategically using the exact words your avatar is searching for. That's how you get discovered, how you stay visible, and how you turn attention into customers.

In the next chapter, we're going to talk about what happens when your captions start working — how to turn those clicks, comments, and conversations into consistent conversions. This is where visibility turns into real money, and where your business shifts from momentum into long-term growth.

CHAPTER 10
YOUR NEXT 90 DAYS STARTS NOW

Why the Next 90 Days Are Crucial

Your first 30 days gave you proof. You learned the system, shared products, and invited your first customers. In Days 31–60, you stacked your income by growing your customer list, sharing proof, and starting to create lead magnets. Now you're entering the most important stretch — Days 61–90.

This is the point where you separate yourself from the crowd. Most people quit before they hit this mark. They dabble, they get distracted, or they convince themselves they need to "start over." That's not you. You've already seen what's possible, and now it's time to cement the habits that turn this from a side hustle into a lifestyle. The next 90 days aren't about trying. They're about proving to yourself that you can build something steady, predictable, and powerful enough to challenge your job.

Think of this chapter as your contract with yourself. If you commit to the process laid out here, the next three months will transform your results.

From Captions to Conversions

In Chapter 9, you learned how to write captions that attract attention using keywords and hooks. That was the first step. But captions don't exist for likes or vanity metrics. Captions exist to convert. A conversion is when someone takes the next step — clicks your link, signs up, joins the system, or buys. That's where your words stop being content and start becoming cash flow.

How does it happen? Simple: your captions are the bridge. A good caption pulls someone in with a hook, explains the value with benefits, and then points them somewhere to act. Without that last piece — the call to action — nothing happens. You'll get attention, maybe even comments, but no momentum. With a clear call to action, every post becomes a pathway back into your circle.

This is where you shift from "posting content" to "building a business." You're no longer just showing up online. You're guiding people to become customers, step by step.

The Daily Formula Refined

At this stage, you should already be familiar with the one-hour-a-day formula from your training modules. But here's how it gets sharpened for the next 90 days:

- **Write and post one caption daily** — keyword-rich, with a hook and call to action.
- **Make 20 meaningful comments per day** — not spam, but genuine comments that spark curiosity about who you are.
- **Go live 2–3 times per week** — use the Show & Tell method. Share your results, your process, or your journey.
- **Share inside the community** — accountability is fuel. Post your wins and lessons learned in the Resell Circle Academy.

This rhythm compounds. One caption might bring a handful of clicks. One live might add two new customers. One comment might open a conversation that turns into a Platinum Plus upgrade a week later. Do it daily for 90 days, and those small moves multiply into consistent growth.

The Power of CTAs (Call to Actions)

If captions are the engine, CTAs are the gas pedal. They move people forward. But here's the mistake most beginners make: they either don't include a CTA at all, or they write weak CTAs that focus on features instead of benefits.

A feature says, "You get a LinkTree page." A benefit says, "You get a page that makes you look like a pro in minutes." A feature says, "The platform has resale rights." A benefit says, "You can start selling products immediately without creating them." Benefits connect to emotion. They connect to what people want: freedom, extra income, security, growth.

When you write your CTAs, make sure they highlight benefits, not just features. And always be specific. Don't say, "Check this out." Say, "Click the link in my bio to learn how to quit your 9-to-5 with resale products."

Here are **20 CTA examples** you can start using right away:

1. “Click the link in my bio and grab your free guide to start earning today.”
2. “DM me the word ‘START’ and I’ll send you the link.”
3. “Comment ‘READY’ if you want the system I’m using.”
4. “Tap the link and see how you can quit your 9-to-5 in 90 days.”
5. “Start your digital income today — the signup link is waiting for you.”
6. “Want to earn while you sleep? Click my invite link to see how.”
7. “Don’t wait for a raise — build your own. Link in bio.”
8. “Join me inside Resell Circle and start stacking income this week.”
9. “Grab your free training now before you overthink it.”
10. “Click the link and discover how to turn ebooks into income.”
11. “The same system that pays me can pay you. Tap the link.”

12. "Stop scrolling and start earning. Link's in my profile."
13. "Take 5 minutes today and set up your business. Start here."
14. "Want proof this works? Check my story, then hit the link."
15. "This is simpler than you think. Get started through my invite."
16. "Freedom starts with one click. Tap the bio link now."
17. "Click through and see how you can resell products you didn't even create."
18. "Stop wasting time. Start building income. Link in profile."
19. "Ready to own your customers for life? Click the link."
20. "Take the first step today — your circle starts here."

Use these as-is or adapt them. The key is always clarity + benefit. Every post should give people a reason to act, not just something to like.

Track Your Progress

In these next 90 days, don't just work blindly. Track what you're doing and what it's producing. Keep count of:

- How many customers you've added to your list.
- How many products you've shared or uploaded.
- How many leads downloaded your freebie.
- How many captions or posts you've written.
- How many times you've gone live.

Even if your numbers feel small, tracking them shows growth. Going from five customers to 25 in 90 days might not sound like a lot — until you remember each one is lifetime-tagged to you, and their activity can generate income for months or years. Numbers build belief, and belief keeps you consistent.

The Legacy of Consistency

By the end of these next 90 days, you'll either still be stuck in the same job cycle or you'll have built proof of an income stream that's growing every week. It won't happen by chance. It will happen because you showed up every day with intent.

Remember what you learned back in Chapter 1: the job mentality trains you to wait for orders, permission, and paychecks. The owner mentality trains you to act daily, whether you feel like it or not. The legacy you create with Resell Circle won't come from one viral post or one lucky sale. It will come from 90 days of stacking, sharing, posting, inviting, and leading.

At that point, you won't just believe this works — you'll have proof. And proof is powerful. Proof keeps you from ever thinking small again.

The Final Challenge

Here's your challenge: commit to the daily formula for the next 90 days. Write one optimized caption with a CTA every day. Make 20 comments. Go live two or three times a week. Share your journey inside the community. Track your growth. Invite creators. Invite customers. Upload your first freebie. Do it without excuses.

Because if you do, you'll never see your job the same way again. You'll look at your paycheck and realize you built something bigger, something better, something you own.

The system is here. The community is here. The training is here. Now it's on you. Ninety days from now, you can look back on this chapter as the moment you decided to stop waiting and start winning. Your circle won't grow if you hesitate — but if you push daily, your circle will change your life.

BEYOND 90 DAYS 10 KEYS TO ACCELERATE YOUR FREEDOM

You've just finished the 90-Day Execution Plan. That alone puts you ahead of most people, because the majority never commit to 90 straight days of consistent action. By now, you've proven to yourself that the system works. You've set up your profile, shared products, invited customers, created content, and learned how to attract the right people. You've built momentum.

But here's the truth: your journey doesn't stop at 90 days. The real opportunity begins after that. Once you've built a foundation, you can start accelerating. Think of Phase One as the "driver's license." You learned how to drive, you practiced the basics, and you got comfortable on the road. Now, Phase Two is about learning how to race, navigate highways, and push your car to its limits. It's the stage where your business stops being fragile and starts becoming unstoppable.

That's what this section is about. *Beyond 90 Days: 10 Keys to Accelerate Your Freedom* is your second gear —

the advanced strategies, insights, and mindset shifts that multiply everything you've already done. None of these keys are "required" to get started. You've already proven you can succeed without them. But if you want to accelerate, scale, and make this lifestyle permanent, these 10 keys are what will keep you ahead of the pack.

Here's what you're about to learn:

1. **The Psychology of Quitting Your Job** — how to handle fear, doubt, and criticism as you transition from employee to entrepreneur.
2. **Money Management for Digital Entrepreneurs** — how to budget, reinvest, and protect your profits so you're building wealth, not just income.
3. **Storytelling That Sells** — why stories build trust faster than sales pitches, and how to share yours effectively.
4. **The 7 Biggest Mistakes Beginners Make** — and how to avoid them before they cost you time and money.
5. **Leverage Other People's Proof Until You Have Your Own** — how to ethically share

wins from the community to build momentum when you're new.

6. **The 30-Day Content Bank** — a ready-to-use library of 30 content ideas you can post immediately.
7. **The Algorithm is Your Business Partner** — how TikTok, Instagram, and YouTube actually push your content, and how to make it work for you.
8. **The Residual Mindset** — shifting from one-time hustles to stacking income that repeats without starting over.
9. **Tools of the Trade** — free and low-cost resources (like Canva, ChatGPT, and LinkTree) that make digital business easier.
10. **How to Build Momentum When Life Gets Busy** — strategies for parents, employees, and part-timers to keep growing in just 30–60 minutes a day.

Each of these chapters is designed to expand what you've already learned. Some are mindset-driven, others are tactical, but all of them serve the same purpose: to accelerate your freedom.

So take a deep breath, celebrate what you've accomplished so far, and then lean in. You've finished the race most people never start. Now it's time to shift gears and see how fast you can really go.

KEY 1
THE PSYCHOLOGY OF QUITTING YOUR JOB

Facing the Fear Factor

The hardest part of leaving a job isn't the paycheck — it's the psychology. From the time we're kids, most of us are taught that jobs equal security. Get good grades, find a good job, and you'll be safe. That conditioning runs deep, and when you start building a business that could replace your income, fear shows up fast. "What if this doesn't work?" "What if I can't pay my bills?" "What if people laugh at me for trying something different?" These questions aren't about logic. They're about fear.

Fear will always whisper in your ear when you're stepping into something bigger. But here's the truth: the job you think is "safe" isn't actually safe at all. Companies lay people off every day. Entire industries shift overnight. One boss's decision can wipe out your security in a matter of hours. The fear you feel about leaving a job isn't really about risk — it's about letting go of conditioning.

Dealing With Doubt and Criticism

It's not just your own doubts you'll face. You'll also face the doubts of the people around you. Family, friends, coworkers — they all have their opinions. Some will say, "That sounds like a scam." Others will say, "You should stick to your job, it's safer." Very few will say, "Go for it, I believe in you."

You have to understand where this comes from. People project their own fears onto you. If they've never stepped into entrepreneurship, they don't know what's possible. They're not really doubting *you* — they're protecting their own comfort zone. If you listen to every critic, you'll never leave the job you claim to hate. The only way to quiet doubt is with results. And results only come if you keep moving despite the noise.

Shifting From Employee to Owner

The biggest psychological shift you'll need to make is moving from the employee mindset to the owner mindset. Employees are trained to wait for orders, to follow rules, and to trade time for money. Owners take initiative, make decisions, and build systems that pay them whether they clock in or not.

That shift can feel uncomfortable at first. You may catch yourself waiting for someone to tell you what to do, or second-guessing whether you're "ready." That's job-thinking showing up again. In this new lane, you don't wait — you decide. You don't ask for permission — you execute. That mental rewiring is the foundation of your freedom.

Building Confidence Through Proof

The fastest way to rewire your psychology is through proof. Not hype, not theory — actual results. The first time you make a commission from sharing a product, your brain says, "This is real." The first time a customer upgrades and you see residual income hit your account, your brain says, "This works." Every small win chips away at the fear and builds confidence.

That's why your goal isn't to make thousands overnight. Your goal is to create proof. Proof changes your psychology. Proof convinces you in ways that no motivational speech ever could. The more proof you stack, the easier it becomes to see yourself as a business owner and not just a job holder.

Embracing the New Normal

Here's the final mental shift: stop treating this business like a side hustle you "hope" will work, and start treating it like your new normal. When you embrace it as normal, you stop apologizing for it. You stop downplaying it. You stop hiding from criticism. Instead, you talk about it with confidence. You share it with conviction. You invite others because you know what you have is real.

That's when everything changes. Because the moment you accept entrepreneurship as your new identity, quitting your job stops being a dream and starts being a timeline.

KEY 2
MONEY MANAGEMENT FOR DIGITAL ENTREPRENEURS

Why Money Management Matters Early

One of the biggest mistakes new entrepreneurs make is thinking that money management can wait until they're making "real money." They tell themselves, "I'll figure it out once the checks get bigger." The problem is, if you don't develop good habits with small income, you'll never manage larger income well either. Bad habits scale just like good ones.

If your goal is to quit your 9-to-5 and live off digital income, then every dollar counts. The way you handle your first $30 commission is the way you'll handle your first $3,000 month. That's why money management isn't something you tack on later — it's a key you put in place right now.

Separate Your Business From Your Life

The first step is simple but critical: separate your business money from your personal money. Open a separate account, even if it's just a no-fee checking account at your bank. Every commission, every payout, every sale should flow there. Why? Because when you mix business money with personal money, you lose clarity. You don't know what's profit, what's expense, or what's left to reinvest.

When you separate accounts, you create a mental and financial boundary. You know exactly what your business is earning, and you can make decisions with confidence. This also sets you up for tax time, where you'll be glad you didn't try to untangle a year's worth of mixed deposits and grocery bills.

Reinvest Before You Reward Yourself

It's tempting to celebrate your first commissions by spending them. And there's nothing wrong with treating yourself a little. But the wisest move is to reinvest first. Think about your business like a fire. The first sparks you create need more wood to grow into a flame. If you pull out the spark and try to warm your whole house with it, it fizzles. But if you feed it, it grows into a steady fire.

Reinvesting could mean upgrading your tools - maybe a Canva Pro subscription, an email autoresponder, or a better microphone for lives. It could also mean boosting your knowledge through training. The point is, your first goal isn't to cash out. It's to grow your capacity to make more.

Budget for the 3 Buckets

A simple framework for managing your digital income is the "three buckets" method:

1. **Reinvestment Bucket (40%)** — This is what you put back into the business. Tools, training, advertising, or anything that fuels growth.
2. **Pay Yourself Bucket (40%)** — This is your reward and motivation. Use it for bills, groceries, or even a fun purchase. Let your business bless your life.
3. **Savings/Taxes Bucket (20%)** — Never forget taxes. Even if your earnings are small at first, setting aside a percentage keeps you from surprises later.

These percentages can flex, but the principle is the same: structure creates freedom. If you don't assign every dollar a job, it disappears without you even noticing.

Think in Residual Terms, Not Just Cash Terms

Most employees think only in cash terms: "I make X dollars per hour." As an entrepreneur, you need to start thinking in residual terms: "This customer could be worth X dollars per month for the next 12 months." That perspective changes how you treat your money. Instead of chasing quick hits, you start building systems that pay you long-term.

This also changes how you view expenses. Buying a $27 subscription might feel like a cost, but if it helps you add three customers worth $40/month in residuals, it's an investment. The key is always asking, "Will this dollar bring back more dollars?" If the answer is yes, it's not an expense. It's growth.

Build Wealth, Not Just Income

Finally, remember that income pays bills, but wealth buys freedom. Don't just spend everything you earn. Save some. Invest some. Use your business income to create breathing room in your life, pay off debt, or build a cushion that gives you peace of mind. The point of this journey isn't just to make digital money — it's to create freedom. Freedom doesn't come from the number of sales you make. It comes from managing those sales wisely so your money keeps working for you long after you've earned it.

KEY 3
STORYTELLING THAT SELLS

Why Stories Beat Sales Pitches

People don't remember ads — they remember stories. You can list all the features of a platform, brag about the income potential, and explain how the system works, but most people will scroll right past it. Why? Because features feel like work. Stories feel like life. Stories connect to emotions, and emotions drive decisions.

When you share your story, you're not just selling a product. You're inviting someone to see themselves in your journey. That's what turns curiosity into trust, and trust into sales. The truth is, most of your audience doesn't want to be "sold." They want to be inspired. And nothing inspires like a story they can relate to.

Your Story Is Enough

One of the biggest myths in marketing is that you need a rags-to-riches story to succeed. You don't. You don't have to be a millionaire or claim you quit your job yesterday. You only need to share your real journey — the struggles, the doubts, the small wins, the breakthroughs.

For example, if you just got your first commission, that's a story. "I made my first $30 online without creating a product, and it feels like proof this works." That story is powerful because it's real, and real is what connects. If you're still in your first month, you can tell a story about what drew you to the platform in the first place: the frustration with your job, the search for something more, the excitement of finally finding a system you can plug into.

The point is, your story doesn't need to be "finished." It just needs to be true. People don't follow perfection. They follow progress.

The Three-Part Story Framework

If you're not sure how to tell your story, here's a simple framework that works every time:

1. **Before** — Describe where you were before Resell Circle. The stress, the long hours, the paycheck-to-paycheck cycle, or the frustration with not having a system.
2. **Discovery** — Share how you found Resell Circle and what made you decide to try it. Keep it short, but make it real.

3. **After/Result** — Show what's changed. It doesn't have to be massive. It could be, "I finally have a system that makes sense," or "I've already got my first customers."

This structure helps people see the transformation. Even if your "after" is small, it gives people hope that they could experience the same thing.

Stories That Sell Without Selling

The beauty of storytelling is that you don't need to push. You don't need to beg. You don't need to sound like a salesperson. When someone hears your story and thinks, "That's me" or "That's what I want," the system sells itself.

Here's a simple example of a caption-story: "Last year, I was frustrated with my job. I felt stuck, but I didn't know how to start something on my own. Then I stumbled across a platform that already had products, a referral system, and a way to build income without creating everything from scratch. I signed up, shared my link, and within days, I saw my first commission. That moment showed me it was possible. Now I'm just following the system and stacking results."

That doesn't sound like a sales pitch, but it's 10x more persuasive than shouting, "Sign up now!"

Keep Collecting New Stories

Your story doesn't end once you've made your first commission. Every milestone becomes another story:

- Your first customer.
- Your first live stream.
- Your first upgrade.
- Your first week of consistent daily action.
- Even your first failure, followed by what you learned.

Each story is a piece of proof. Collect them. Share them. The more stories you tell, the more your audience sees you as real, relatable, and trustworthy.

Turning Your Story Into Sales

At the end of every story, always connect it to a call to action (CTA). This is where storytelling meets sales. Don't just say, "Here's what happened." Add, "If you're ready to start your own journey, click the link in my bio." That way, your story inspires action.

Stories sell because they bypass resistance. They're not about convincing. They're about showing. And when you show people the path, they naturally want to follow.

KEY 4
THE 7 BIGGEST MISTAKES BEGINNERS MAKE

Why Mistakes Matter

Every new entrepreneur makes mistakes. That's normal. The difference between those who succeed and those who quit is how they respond to those mistakes. Some people let small errors discourage them and stop their momentum. Others treat mistakes as lessons, adjust quickly, and keep going. If you know the most common pitfalls before you start, you can avoid wasting time, money, and energy. Consider this chapter your "warning signs on the road." They're not here to scare you. They're here to keep you on track.

Mistake #1: Overcomplicating the Process

Many beginners think they need to reinvent the wheel. They try to build fancy funnels, design logos for weeks, or launch a dozen social media pages before they've even made their first sale. That's job-thinking again — stalling with busywork. The system is already built. Your job is to plug in, share, and grow. Simplicity wins. Complexity kills momentum.

Mistake #2: Waiting Too Long to Share

Fear of judgment keeps people silent. They think, "I'll start posting once I know everything," or, "I'll wait until I have big results." That delay costs them time and customers. The truth is, your audience doesn't expect perfection. They want honesty. If you just got started, say that. If you just made your first $30, celebrate it. Share where you are right now. Waiting until you feel "ready" is how most people never start.

Mistake #3: Ignoring Training

Resell Circle gives you six training modules plus community mentorship. Yet some people skip it and try to figure everything out themselves. That's like being handed a map and choosing to wander in circles. Training accelerates you. It answers questions you don't even know to ask yet. Every successful member leans into training because they know information is leverage.

Mistake #4: Quitting Too Soon

This one hurts the most. People quit right before the breakthrough. They make a few posts, invite a couple of people, face a little rejection, and then say, "This doesn't work." In reality, they just didn't stay long enough to see results. Business isn't microwaved. It's baked. If you give it consistent action for 90 days, you'll have proof. But if you quit in week two, you'll never know what was waiting for you.

Mistake #5: Comparing to Others

Comparison is poison. You'll see someone who has more followers, more sales, or more confidence on camera, and you'll think, "I could never be like that." What you don't see are the months or years they spent building those skills. Your journey is your journey. Comparing your Day 1 to someone else's Year 3 is a guaranteed way to feel defeated. Focus on your lane. Celebrate your small wins. Thcy add up.

Mistake #6: Treating It Like a Hobby

If you treat this business like a hobby, it will pay you like one. If you treat it like a business, it will pay you like one. That means setting goals, scheduling time, tracking results, and holding yourself accountable. Hobbies are optional. Businesses require discipline. The system is built to reward owners, not dabblers.

Mistake #7: Forgetting the Customer is for Life

The last mistake is the most expensive: forgetting that every customer you invite is tagged to you for life. Beginners sometimes chase the next person so fast that they forget to nurture the ones they already have. But here's the power: when one of your customers buys from anyone on the platform, you still earn. That means your existing customers are just as valuable as new ones. Treat them well. Engage them. Support them. Don't neglect the lifetime value sitting right in front of you.

Learn, Don't Repeat

Mistakes aren't the end of the road. They're simply signals. If you overcomplicated things last month, simplify this month. If you quit posting last week, start fresh today. If you've been comparing yourself, shift your focus back to your own path. The only real failure is refusing to learn.

If you avoid these seven pitfalls — or better yet, learn from them early — you'll save yourself months of frustration. You'll also set yourself apart from the majority of people who give up before they see results. Success isn't about being perfect. It's about staying consistent and correcting course when you drift.

KEY 5
LEVERAGE OTHER PEOPLE'S PROOF UNTIL YOU HAVE YOUR OWN

Why Proof Matters

In the online world, proof is everything. People are skeptical. They've seen too many empty promises, too many scams, too many "get rich quick" pitches that never delivered. So when they hear about a new platform or system, their first thought isn't excitement — it's doubt. "Does this really work?"

The fastest way to answer that question isn't with theory or hype. It's with proof. Proof makes things real. Proof takes something that sounds like a dream and turns it into something believable. The problem is, when you're just starting, you might not have your own proof yet. That's where the power of community comes in.

Borrowing Belief from Others

One of the smartest moves you can make early on is leveraging other people's proof. If someone else in the community just made a sale, that's proof. If someone else quit their job, that's proof. If someone else got their first customer in the first week, that's proof. And because Resell Circle is structured as a community-driven platform, their wins reflect what's possible for you too.

When you share those stories, you're not lying. You're not pretending. You're simply saying, "Look what's happening inside this system I'm part of." That's completely honest — and it builds belief while you're still creating your own track record.

How to Share Proof Ethically

There's a right way and a wrong way to share other people's proof. The wrong way is claiming it as your own. Never do that. If someone in the community posts about making $500, don't repost and say, "Look what I made." That's dishonest and it will backfire.

The right way is to frame it in context. For example:

- "I just joined Resell Circle, and here's what other members are already experiencing…"
- "I'm still new, but I've seen people inside this platform make their first sales within days."
- "This is why I joined — the system is already producing results for people, and I'm learning step by step to do the same."

Notice the shift. You're positioning yourself as part of a winning community, while still being transparent about your own journey.

The Transition Point: From Borrowed Proof to Personal Proof

Here's the exciting part: when you borrow proof, it won't be long before you start creating your own. And when you do, your credibility multiplies. The first time you share your dashboard screenshot, your first commission, or your first upgrade, your audience will remember: "This person has been showing me this system works — and now it's working for them too." That's powerful.

So don't see borrowing proof as weakness. See it as a bridge. It bridges the gap between getting started and stacking your own results.

Keep Collecting Stories

Even after you have your own proof, never stop leveraging the stories of others. Because your audience isn't just made up of people like you — it's diverse. Some people will relate to your journey, while others may resonate more with someone else's. Maybe you're a parent and your story inspires other parents. But a young student might connect better to the story of another student who made their first $200 online.

The more stories you share, the more people can see themselves in the system. Proof multiplies belief, and belief multiplies customers.

Proof Creates Movement

At the end of the day, proof is what drives people to act. You can talk about potential all you want, but potential doesn't move people. Proof does. That's why it's not only okay to share other people's wins — it's smart. As you grow, combine borrowed proof with your own, and you'll have a steady stream of stories that inspire belief and drive action.

KEY 6
THE 30-DAY CONTENT BANK

Why Consistency Beats Perfection

One of the biggest reasons people stall in digital business is running out of things to post. They start strong for a week, then hit a wall: "What do I say today?" That silence kills momentum faster than anything else. The truth is, content doesn't need to be perfect. It just needs to be consistent.

Think of your content like drops of water. One drop doesn't do much. But drip every day for 30 days, and suddenly you've carved a groove. That groove is trust. It's recognition. It's momentum. The problem isn't lack of ability — it's lack of ideas. That's why I've created a 30-day content bank you can draw from anytime you feel stuck.

How to Use This Content Bank

This isn't about copying word-for-word. It's about sparking ideas. Read each prompt, adapt it to your story, your journey, and your voice. If you use these for 30 straight days, you'll not only stay consistent, you'll also train your brain to see content opportunities everywhere. Soon, you won't be asking, "What should I post?" You'll be saying, "I have too many ideas."

30 Days of Content Prompts

Here's your month-long bank of ideas. Each one can be a caption, a short video, a live, or even a story post:

1. Share why you started this journey (your "before" story).
2. Post about your first small win (first customer, first $30, first share).
3. Record a 30-second video explaining what digital products are.
4. Share a testimonial from someone in the community.
5. Post about what freedom means to you.
6. Share a behind-the-scenes of your setup (workspace, profile, training).
7. Answer a common question: "Do I need followers to start?"
8. Post your favorite motivational quote and tie it to your journey.

9. Share a screenshot of your training modules and say what you're learning.
10. Post about the difference between job income and residual income.
11. Share your first piece of proof (a notification, a new customer).
12. Post about how Resell Circle saves time compared to building from scratch.
13. Go live and tell your "why."
14. Share the top 3 benefits of resale rights in simple words.
15. Post about a mistake you made and what you learned.
16. Record a short "myth vs. truth" video about digital income.
17. Share someone else's success story from the platform.
18. Post a quick how-to tip (like setting up your profile picture).
19. Share your 90-day goal publicly.
20. Post a screenshot of your LinkTree and explain why it's powerful.

21. Do a comparison post: "Job paycheck vs. digital income."
22. Record a short clip about how customers are tracked for life.
23. Post about what excites you most about your journey.
24. Share a tip from Module 6 (hour-a-day strategy).
25. Post about the importance of consistency over perfection.
26. Share a photo of you watching a training or reading.
27. Do a "3 things I learned this week" post.
28. Share an invite link with a CTA: "Start with me today."
29. Record a quick "day in the life" clip.
30. Celebrate finishing 30 days of content and invite others to start their 30 days.

Why This Works

Notice how this list blends personal stories, proof, education, and motivation. That's the mix your audience needs. If you only post motivation, you'll inspire but not convert. If you only post proof, you'll look like a brag board. If you only post education, you'll sound like a teacher, not a guide. The blend makes you real. And real is what sells.

Build Your Own Bank

Once you use this list, start building your own. Every question someone asks you, every small win you hit, every insight you learn can be turned into content. Save those ideas in a notes app. Soon, you'll have your own 60-day, 90-day, even 180-day bank of content. That's when content creation stops being stressful and starts being natural.

KEY 7
THE ALGORITHM IS YOUR BUSINESS PARTNER

Stop Fighting the Algorithm

Most people talk about social media algorithms like they're the enemy. "The algorithm is against me." "The algorithm killed my reach." That mindset is a mistake. The algorithm isn't against you — it just doesn't know you yet. Think of the algorithm as an employee who only promotes what you consistently show up with. If you treat it like a partner and feed it the right signals, it will work for you 24/7, putting your content in front of people you could never reach on your own.

Instead of complaining about what the algorithm didn't do, start focusing on what you can do to work with it.

What the Algorithm Wants

Every platform — TikTok, Instagram, YouTube, even Facebook — runs on the same principle: keep people engaged. The longer people stay on the platform, the more ads get shown, the more money the company makes. That means the algorithm rewards content that makes people stop, watch, like, share, or comment.

When you understand this, you stop guessing. You know that if you post consistently, if you hook people in the first few seconds, and if your content sparks engagement, the algorithm will reward you. It doesn't care if you're new or established. It only cares if your content keeps people on the app.

Consistency Over Virality

Too many beginners chase virality — one post that blows up, one video that gets a million views. But algorithms don't reward one-hit wonders; they reward consistency. Posting once a month won't teach the algorithm who you are or who should see you. Posting daily or near-daily sends a signal: "This account is active, reliable, and worth showing to more people."

Think of it like trust. The more you post, the more the algorithm trusts you. And once it trusts you, it starts recommending you to audiences beyond your followers. That's where organic growth comes from.

Signals That Boost Your Reach

Here are the signals algorithms love — the things you can control:

- **Watch Time**: If people watch your video to the end, or even rewatch it, the algorithm takes notice.
- **Engagement**: Likes, comments, shares, and saves tell the platform your content is valuable.
- **Keywords in Captions**: Just like we covered in Chapter 9, platforms now scan your words. If your caption includes "digital products" and someone searches that, your content has a better chance of showing up.
- **Consistency**: Daily posts give more data points to the algorithm, which increases your chances of hitting bigger reach.

You don't need to master every detail of how algorithms work. You just need to consistently give them the signals they love.

Partner With the Algorithm

The best way to think about algorithms is as free employees. You create content; they deliver it to the right people. But they only "work" if you keep showing up.

Imagine hiring an employee and only giving them one hour of work every month. They wouldn't know what to do with themselves. That's what happens when you post inconsistently.

But if you give the algorithm a steady flow of posts, captions, and signals, it becomes your most loyal business partner. It never sleeps. It never takes a day off. It just keeps delivering your content, finding your audience, and building your reach.

Trust the Process

Don't expect instant results. Algorithms take time to learn who your audience is and what your content means. At first, you may only reach a handful of people. But if you stay consistent, those handfuls turn into hundreds, then thousands. Most people quit before they reach that tipping point. Don't be one of them. Stay consistent long enough for the algorithm to trust you — and it will open doors you couldn't imagine.

KEY 8
THE RESIDUAL MINDSET

The Difference Between One-Time Money and Residual Money

Most people are trained to think in terms of one-time money. You work a shift, you get paid once. You sell a product, you get paid once. It's a cycle of starting over every time you want to earn again. Residual income flips that script. Instead of starting from zero each day, you stack streams of income that keep flowing long after the initial work is done.

Think of it like planting seeds. A one-time sale is like buying a piece of fruit at the store — once you eat it, it's gone. Residual income is like planting a tree. You water it once, and it keeps giving fruit season after season. The difference isn't just financial — it's psychological. When you build with a residual mindset, you stop asking, "How much did I make today?" and start asking, "What seeds did I plant that will pay me tomorrow, next month, and even next year?"

Why Residuals Change Everything

Residual income is freedom income. It's the type of money that allows you to take a day off, spend time with your family, or even sleep — and still wake up to new earnings. It takes away the pressure of always having to chase the next sale or the next hour of work. That's why Resell Circle is built around multiple residual streams. Every customer you invite, every subscription you generate, every referral you bring in becomes a seed that can keep paying you.

Without a residual mindset, you'll always be stuck in hustle mode. With it, you can build a life where your time and your money finally separate — and that's where freedom begins.

Think Ownership, Not Just Sales

Residuals are tied to ownership. Inside Resell Circle, every customer you bring in is tagged to you for life. That means even if they don't buy from you directly, you still benefit when they buy from others. That's ownership.

So instead of chasing one-off sales like most digital hustlers do, your focus should be on building ownership. Every customer you add, every creator you invite, every subscription you secure is long-term equity in your circle. Don't think like a cashier making a single transaction. Think like a landlord who collects rent every month, whether or not they pick up the phone that day.

Small Residuals Add Up

The mistake most people make is underestimating small residuals. They think, "It's only $10" or "It's only $40." But stack those numbers across dozens or hundreds of customers, and suddenly you have rent money, car money, or even quit-your-job money. Residual income isn't flashy at first. It's steady. And steady beats flashy every time.

Remember this: your job gives you a paycheck. Your circle gives you a pipeline. A paycheck ends when you stop showing up. A pipeline keeps flowing even when life happens.

Building the Residual Mindset Daily

Here's how to put the residual mindset into practice:

- **Value customers for life, not just one sale.** Every customer is long-term. Treat them that way.

- **Prioritize subscriptions and referrals.** They're your monthly seeds. Plant as many as you can.
- **Track growth in months, not just days.** Ask yourself, "What did I do this month to grow my pipeline?"
- **Celebrate small wins.** That $27 monthly subscription isn't small — it's proof of freedom stacking.

Residual income doesn't come from hustling harder. It comes from thinking smarter, building ownership, and staying consistent long enough for the seeds you plant to grow.

KEY 9
TOOLS OF THE TRADE

Why Tools Matter

Building a digital business without the right tools is like trying to build a house with your bare hands. You might get something up eventually, but it'll take forever, it'll be sloppy, and you'll burn out before you finish. Tools don't replace the work — they make the work easier, faster, and more effective. The good news is, in today's digital age, you don't need expensive equipment or a giant budget. With just a handful of free or low-cost tools, you can run your business like a pro from your phone or laptop.

Canva: Design Without Being a Designer

Most beginners get stuck thinking they need to hire a graphic designer for everything. Canva changes that. Canva lets you create flyers, ebooks, social media posts, and product covers in minutes — with drag-and-drop templates anyone can use. Need a professional-looking ebook cover? Canva. Need a quick Instagram post? Canva. Even with the free version, you can create content that looks polished and trustworthy. It's not about being fancy; it's about being consistent and professional.

ChatGPT: Your 24/7 Content Assistant

If Canva makes you look good, ChatGPT helps you sound good. Writer's block is one of the biggest enemies of consistency. ChatGPT solves that by giving you instant ideas, captions, hooks, scripts, and even full product drafts. The secret is in the prompts you give it. Ask specific questions like, "Write me a TikTok caption about digital products with the keywords passive income and financial freedom." In seconds, you'll have something to work with. Use ChatGPT as your brainstorming partner, your copywriting assistant, and your idea generator.

LinkTree: Keep It All in One Place

People online have short attention spans. If you tell them, "DM me for the link," or "Scroll through my profile," you'll lose most of them. That's why LinkTree (or Resell Circle's built-in link system) is powerful. It gives you one simple link where all your important pages live — your invite link, your freebie, your products, your social media. Instead of scattering your audience across platforms, you point them to one hub. Simplicity creates action.

Zoom: Build Connection Through Conversation

Business isn't just about clicks and captions. It's about connection. Zoom calls let you build real relationships with your audience, your team, and your mentors. Inside Resell Circle, mentorship calls and live trainings happen on Zoom for a reason — because nothing replaces face-to-face energy, even if it's digital. Hosting your own small calls down the line can also be a game-changer. One 20-minute call with a potential customer can do more than 20 posts.

Other Helpful Freebies

A few more free or affordable tools to keep in your pocket:

- **Google Docs & Sheets**: For planning, writing, and tracking your progress.
- **Screen recorders** (like Loom or built-in phone apps): Perfect for tutorials or showing proof.

- **Social schedulers** (like Buffer or Meta Business Suite): Let you schedule posts so you stay consistent even on busy days.

None of these tools replace action. But they remove excuses. When you have Canva for design, ChatGPT for words, LinkTree for links, and Zoom for connection, you're running a streamlined business most people would've killed for just 10 years ago.

Tools Are Leverage, Not Crutches

Don't fall into the trap of thinking tools do the work for you. They don't. They just make your work more efficient. Canva won't make you consistent. ChatGPT won't make you disciplined. LinkTree won't invite customers for you. You're still the driver. The tools are just the car. Use them wisely, and they'll take you farther, faster, with less stress. Ignore them, and you'll work harder than you need to.

At the end of the day, tools won't build your circle. But the right tools in the right hands will multiply your reach, polish your presence, and help you scale without burning out.

KEY 10
HOW TO BUILD MOMENTUM WHEN LIFE GETS BUSY

Life Won't Slow Down for You

One of the biggest lies people tell themselves is, "I'll start when things calm down." The truth? Life never calms down. Work deadlines, family needs, unexpected bills, even simple exhaustion — something will always compete for your time and energy. If you wait for the "perfect" moment to build your digital business, you'll wait forever. The key isn't waiting for life to slow down. The key is learning how to keep momentum even when life feels chaotic.

The Power of Micro-Actions

When life is heavy, you don't need to work eight hours a day. You just need to keep moving. Small, consistent actions create more momentum than rare, massive ones. If you only have 20 minutes, write a caption. If you only have 10 minutes, make a comment or two on posts. If you have 5 minutes, share your link. Micro-actions stack. One day you'll look back and realize those tiny steps added up to a big result.

Momentum isn't about intensity. It's about consistency. A dripping faucet eventually fills a bucket.

Protecting Your Non-Negotiables

When life is busy, your schedule gets messy. That's why you need non-negotiables — small daily commitments you don't skip, no matter what. Maybe it's one post per day. Maybe it's 20 comments. Maybe it's showing up on a mentorship call once a week. Pick your non-negotiables and protect them. Even if you can't do everything, do those.

Think of it like brushing your teeth. No matter how busy you are, you don't skip it. Why? Because you know the long-term cost if you do. Treat your non-negotiables the same way. They keep your business healthy, even when life is unpredictable.

Leverage Community When You Can't Carry It Alone

Busy seasons aren't meant to be carried alone. That's where the Resell Circle community comes in. Plug into mentorship calls. Lean on training modules. Share your struggles in the Academy. Sometimes just knowing you're not the only one juggling chaos can give you the strength to push through.

And here's the secret: when you share honestly about being busy but still showing up, your audience respects you more. They see you're human. They see you're consistent even when it's tough. That authenticity builds trust faster than pretending you have it all together.

Reframe "Busy" as an Advantage

Instead of seeing your busy schedule as a barrier, reframe it as proof. Think about it: if you can grow your business in the middle of a busy life, your audience can too. Share that. Let them see your kids running in the background of a live. Let them hear that you're building this before or after your 9-to-5. That relatability makes your journey even more powerful. You're not just teaching business. You're showing resilience.

Keep the Long Game in Mind

When life piles up, it's easy to think, "Maybe I should just quit and try again later." Don't. Remember why you started: to quit the cycle of paycheck-to-paycheck, to own your time, to create residuals that work while you live. Quitting when you're busy only guarantees you'll stay stuck in the same busy cycle forever.

Instead, keep the long game in mind. Busy seasons pass. But if you stay consistent during them, your business won't just survive — it'll grow stronger. Every action you take while busy is proof that you can handle this. Proof that your excuses aren't bigger than your vision.

THE 90-DAY ACTION PLAN

PART ONE: TRAINING & LEARNING TRACKER

This section mirrors the mentorship modules (1–6) found on the Resell Circle Platform. Each module gets its own checklist space, with a "✓ Watched," "Notes," and "Takeaway" line.

Module 1: Getting Started — Launch Your Digital Business in 10 Minutes

- ☐ Watched Video
- Key Notes:

  ____

  ____

  ____

  ____

  ____

  ____

  ____

  ____

- My Takeaway:

  ____

  ____

  ____

Module 2: Set Up Your LinkTree & Tools to Earn More

- ☐ Watched Video
- Key Notes:
- My Takeaway:

Module 3: Social Media Setup to Attract Real Buyers

- ☐ Watched Video
- Key Notes:

  ____
  ____
  ____
  ____
  ____
  ____
  ____
  ____

- My Takeaway:

  ____
  ____
  ____
  ____
  ____
  ____
  ____

Module 4: Big Commissions — How to Maximize Resell Circle

- ☐ Watched Video
- Key Notes:

  ____
  ____
  ____
  ____
  ____
  ____

- My Takeaway:

Module 5: How to Attract Your Ideal Customers

- ☐ Watched Video
- Key Notes:

- My Takeaway:

Module 6: Launch Your 5-Day Challenge & Get Paid

- ☐ Watched Video
- Key Notes:

  ____

  ____

  ____

  ____

  ____

  ____

  ____

  ____
- My Takeaway:

  ____

  ____

  ____

  ____

  ____

  ____

  ____

PART TWO: EXECUTION & GOAL TRACKER

1. Campaigns — Track Where Your Traffic Comes From

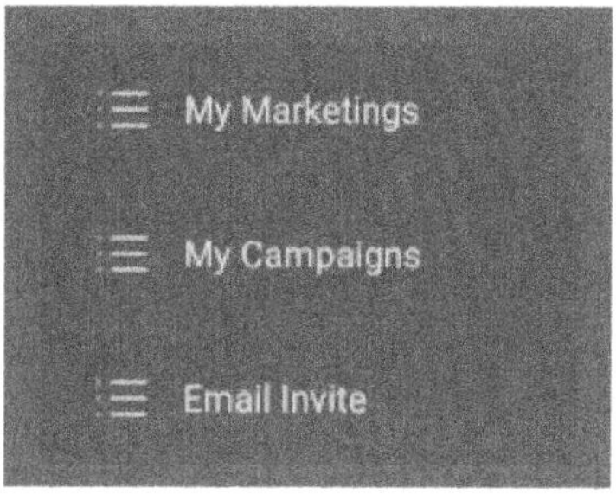

Inside Resell Circle, every marketing campaign starts with a link. You can take your invite link or landing page link, profile page, etc., and then use the **Campaign Tool** to add a unique code. This tells you exactly where your clicks and customers are coming from.

For example:

- Create a link tagged **?cid=MTU=** and share it on Facebook.
- Create a link tagged **?cid=MYA=** and post it in Instagram Stories.
- Create a link tagged **?cid=MFD=** if you're testing a Twitter/X ad.

Now when traffic flows in, you'll know precisely which platform or campaign is performing best. No guessing — just clear data.

Checklist:

- ☐ Created my first campaign
- Campaign Name: ______________________
- Where I Posted It: ____________________
- Results: ______________________________

https://resellcircle.com/MillionaireAL/invite

2. Goals — Track Your Progress

Write down your goals, check them off as you complete them, and watch your momentum grow. Every box you tick is proof that your business is moving forward.

Examples of Goals You Can Set:

- ☐ Get my first 5 customers into the system
- ☐ Sell my first digital product
- ☐ Earn my first $100 in commissions
- ☐ Host my first live video using Show & Tell formula
- ☐ Reach 100 unique clicks on my invite link
- ☐ Complete all 6 mentorship modules and take notes

- ☐ Upload my first custom digital product
- ☐ Share my LinkTree on all social platforms
- ☐ Set up my first marketing campaign in the dashboard
- ☐ Post 20 comments in groups or communities
- ☐ Reach 1,000 total unique link clicks
- ☐ Earn my first $500 in cumulative commissions
- ☐ Invite a creator to upload their own products
- ☐ Grow to 25 total customers in my system
- ☐ Sell a resale rights or PLR product for the first time
- ☐ Create and share my first lead magnet
- ☐ Attend 3 live Zoom mentorship calls
- ☐ Post proof of results (screenshot or story) publicly
- ☐ Earn my first $1,000 in cumulative commissions
- ☐ Build a 90-day routine (1 post, 20 comments daily)

Use the space below to write your own goals:

My Goal: ______________________________
Target Completion Date: ___________________
Result / Notes: __________________________

My Goal: ______________________________
Target Completion Date: ________________
Result / Notes: _________________________

My Goal: ______________________________
Target Completion Date: ________________
Result / Notes: _________________________

My Goal: ______________________________
Target Completion Date: ________________
Result / Notes: _________________________

My Goal: ______________________________
Target Completion Date: ________________
Result / Notes: _________________________

My Goal: ______________________________
Target Completion Date: ________________
Result / Notes: _________________________

My Goal: ______________________________
Target Completion Date: ________________
Result / Notes: _________________________

My Goal: ______________________________
Target Completion Date: ________________
Result / Notes: _________________________

My Goal: ______________________________
Target Completion Date: ________________
Result / Notes: _________________________

My Goal: ______________________________
Target Completion Date: ____________________
Result / Notes: __________________________

My Goal: ______________________________
Target Completion Date: ____________________
Result / Notes: __________________________

My Goal: ______________________________
Target Completion Date: ____________________
Result / Notes: __________________________

My Goal: ______________________________
Target Completion Date: ____________________
Result / Notes: __________________________

My Goal: ______________________________
Target Completion Date: ____________________
Result / Notes: __________________________

My Goal: ______________________________
Target Completion Date: ____________________
Result / Notes: __________________________

My Goal: ______________________________
Target Completion Date: ____________________
Result / Notes: __________________________

My Goal: ______________________________
Target Completion Date: ____________________
Result / Notes: __________________________

My Goal: ______________________________________
Target Completion Date: ________________________
Result / Notes: _________________________________

My Goal: ______________________________________
Target Completion Date: ________________________
Result / Notes: _________________________________

My Goal: ______________________________________
Target Completion Date: ________________________
Result / Notes: _________________________________

My Goal: ______________________________________
Target Completion Date: ________________________
Result / Notes: _________________________________

YOUR FREE BONUS LIBRARY

When you join Resell Circle today, you'll also unlock **five powerful bonus guides** at no extra cost. Each one is designed to help you hit the ground running, master the platform, and accelerate your results. From your first $500 to building long-term recurring income, these resources are waiting inside your account the moment you sign up.

Bonus #1

How to Make Your First $500 on Resell Circle

This beginner-friendly ebook walks you through the exact steps to start earning on Resell Circle—no guesswork, no overwhelm.

Whether you're brand new or haven't made your first sale yet, this guide helps you focus on the 20% of actions that bring 80% of the results.

You’ll learn how to:

- ▶ Set up your profile and unlock earning features fast
- ▶ Share done-for-you products using lifetime tracking links
- ▶ Use your Linktree and landing pages to get traffic
- ▶ Promote without being pushy or needing a big audience
- ▶ Earn from multiple streams: books, upgrades, and referrals

You’ll also discover:

- ✅ What to say in your first social media post
- ✅ How to follow up without being annoying
- ✅ Where your $500+ in earnings can realistically come from
- ✅ A checklist for your first 7 days to stay focused

This is the Resell Circle jumpstart guide. If you want results fast, this bonus will help you stay clear, confident, and ready to win.

Your first $500 online might just start right here.

Bonus #2

How to Quit Your 9-to-5 in 90 Days

This powerful blueprint shows you how to escape the 9-to-5 grind and start building real residual income using the done-for-you Resell Circle platform.

It's not about hype or quick fixes. This book gives you a step-by-step execution plan that shows you exactly how to treat Resell Circle like a business, pace yourself for 90 days, and stack income streams that grow month after month.

Inside, you'll discover how to:

- ▶ Kill the job mentality and think like an owner
- ▶ Leverage a done-for-you system that pays multiple ways
- ▶ Set up your profile, start training, and invite customers
- ▶ Use the 90-day blueprint to build real momentum
- ▶ Transition into long-term growth with lifetime customer ownership

You'll also get:

- ✅ A simple plan to replace job thinking with business building
- ✅ Training insights and a checklist to stay on track
- ✅ Two phases: the 90-day plan + 10 keys to accelerate freedom

This is more than a guide — it's your playbook for turning Resell Circle into a real income system.

Follow it step by step and start building your freedom today.

Bonus #3

Launch Your Digital Products With Sales Psychology That Profits

This beginner-friendly guide is packed with real templates, swipe files, and simple steps to help you launch and sell digital products like a pro.

If you've ever wanted to create and sell digital products—but didn't know where to start—this is the shortcut you've been looking for.

You'll learn how to:

- ▶ Come up with winning product ideas—even if you're "not creative"
- ▶ Write product descriptions that get people to buy
- ▶ Build sales pages that lead customers step-by-step to "yes"
- ▶ Use sales psychology tricks without feeling salesy or fake
- ▶ Price your products, promote them, and attract affiliates

You’re also getting ready-made swipe files, including:

- ✅ Proven sales page outlines
- ✅ 20 fill-in-the-blank CTA phrases
- ✅ Description formulas that convert
- ✅ Upsell/downsell templates
- ✅ Bonus ideas that increase perceived value
- ✅ Lead magnet formats that attract buyers—not just freebie seekers

This is not fluff. It’s the same marketing system used by six- and seven-figure creators—simplified for first-time launchers.

Follow the steps, use the tools, and launch your first product with confidence.

Bonus #4

Make Big Profits With Your Own Digital Product

This planner-style workbook gives you the complete blueprint for building and launching a profitable digital product—no audience, fancy website, or tech background required.

Whether you've got experience, a skill, or just a story to share, this guide shows you how to turn it into a product that sells.

Inside, you'll learn how to:

- ▶ Identify a profitable digital product idea from your life or skillset
- ▶ Define your niche and ideal audience for maximum sales
- ▶ Structure your product using the 5-part transformation model
- ▶ Price your product confidently using proven value formulas
- ▶ Prepare and launch without overthinking or stalling out

You'll also get:

- ✅ Worksheets to plan your product and message
- ✅ Sales page checklists and launch messaging templates
- ✅ A weekly content rhythm to stay visible and grow sales

This guide is clear, direct, and packed with examples to help you go from idea to income—fast.

It's your step-by-step action plan to turn knowledge into profit.

Bonus #5

How to Build a Subscription-Based Income in 14 Days

This powerful action guide walks you step-by-step through creating a digital subscription that pays you month after month—even if you're just getting started.

Inside, you'll learn how to build reliable, recurring income using either your own products or the Resell Circle platform as your base.

You'll learn how to:

- ▶ Create your first $20/month subscription—even with no audience
- ▶ Craft a value stack that feels worth $200+
- ▶ Plug into Resell Circle for instant recurring commissions
- ▶ Deliver your offer with clarity, confidence, and structure
- ▶ Scale your subscriber base from 10 to 50+ in 90 days

Plus, you'll get:

- ✅ 14-day launch plan with daily actions
- ✅ Templates to outline your offer and pricing
- ✅ Examples of real subscription success paths
- ✅ Done-for-you Resell Circle use cases to get started instantly

Whether you build your own program or plug into an existing system, this guide shows you how to create lasting income with just one customer—who pays you every single month.

Start building predictable digital income today—with a system that grows as you do.

Made in the USA
Monee, IL
04 November 2026

67377405R00095